BEGAM SAMRU

BEGAM SAMRU

By

BRAJENDRANATH BANERJI

WITH A FOREWORD BY

JADUNATH SARKAR, M.A., I.E.S.

GYAN

Published by

Gyan Publishing House
5, Ansari Road
Daryaganj, New Delhi-110002
Phone: 011-47034999, 9811692060
E-mail: books@gyanbooks.com

Distribution Network
gyanbooks.com
India, USA, Canada, UK, Australia, France

ISBN : 978-81-212-6659-8 (PB)
First Published, 1925

2nd Impression 2022

Printed at: Gyan Press, Delhi.

BEGAM SAMRU
Author: BRAJENDRANATH BANERJI

BEGAM SAMRU

BY

BRAJENDRANATH BANERJI

WITH A FOREWORD BY

JADUNATH SARKAR, M.A., I.E.S.

1925

To

KRISHNASHEKHAR BOSE, Esq.

THIS BOOK IS DEDICATED

AS A TOKEN OF SINCERE REGARD

FOREWORD

Hindustan during the second half of the 18th century presents a sad spectacle to the Indian patriot and a perplexing problem to the historian.

The vitality of the Mughal empire had been inwardly sapped at Aurangzib's death at the beginning of the century, but its outward show continued to impose on the world for 50 years more. Nadir Shah gave a rude shock to the Delhi throne in 1739, but things seemed to go on as before for some years afterwards. At last the death of the Emperor Muhammad Shah and the great Nizam Asaf Jah, both in 1748, removed the last recognized heads of the old order. Then followed a new era of rapid political revolutions, wars of succession, murder and usurpation, dismemberment of the empire, and rise of petty chiefs to independence everywhere. In Southern India, too, the death of the Chhatrapati Shahu, which followed next year (1749), introduced the element of dissolution; the unifying central power of the Maratha State was gone; and though there was no provincial independence for 25 years more, the increasing failure of the Court of Puna to keep the Maratha generals in the far off provinces under control betrayed unmistakably the weakening of the legitimate authority of the State.

Into this disintegrating world entered the Europeans,—no longer the humble merchants that they had been for a century and more in the past, but as warriors and arbiters of India's political destiny. As the eighteenth century wore on, it became increasingly clear that the decisive factor in the unceasing struggles among the countless Indian princes was command over European military talent. European captains began to dominate the politics of India by serving as free-lances, training native troops in European discipline and leading them in action for their Indian masters; and finally one of these European nations dropped the mask, swept aside the puppet native princes, and became the undisputed master of India.

The period between the death of the old Emperor Muhammad Shah (1748) and the establishment of British suzerainty under Wellesley (1803) was a golden age to foreign mercenaries in India, but not in a political sense. There was still a nominal Padishah of Delhi, whose name might be invoked as the final legitimate authority. But the actual sovereign power,—outside the fringe areas of Bengal and Madras (then under English control) and the extreme south (under the house of Haidar Ali),—was ambitiously snatched at by the Marathas, who rushed in to seize the heritage of the unworthy successors of Akbar and Shah Jahan. The Maratha dream of an Indian empire was shattered at Panipat (1761), and though that race recovered its predominance in the central part of Northern India two decades later, it was merely as a provincial Power, not recognized as paramount by the other Powers in the land. The newly revived Maratha predominance at Delhi depended on the genius of one man, Mahadji Sindhia, and disappeared with the death of that great leader.

The normal condition of nearly all India during this half century was that of ever-changing alliances and wars, the sudden growth and as sudden shrinking of an immense number of separate principalities, whose ambition and instability made them entirely dependent on military adventurers possessed of enterprising spirit and organizing power. Where there was no patriotic policy and no national army, a European-led regiment could raise a petty native chieftain to a royal throne or open to him the gates of a treasure-laden imperial fort. Naturally, in such a world all the wealth of the grateful prince, all the treasure-hoard of the sacked fortress would be the reward of the triumphant European captain.

Thus the history of Hindustan under the free-lances is a volume of fascinating adventures and romantic personalities, where the wealth and beauty of the land and positions of independent command lay as the ready prizes of the cool head and the daring heart, without any need for high birth or legal title. Among these adventurers none has left a more wonderful life-story than a woman,—a Kashmiri girl who from abject poverty and obscurity rose to the command of a European-drilled brigade, the sovereignty of a territory as large as two English counties, and the honoured position of a shield to the Delhi imperial family, and died in the fulness of her years in the odour of sanctity as the honoured ally and social associate of the English rulers and a saint of the Roman Catholic Church!

Such was Begam Samru. Her career, made up of truths stranger than the most imaginative romance, has attracted many a pen in the past. But the present work by Mr. Brajendranath Banerji is the first attempt to write her biography on the basis of a critical study of *all* the available historical materials in print or manuscript. I have supplied him with all the contemporary records about the Begam in Persian French and Marathi; he has himself utilized all the printed English works on the subject and spent many months in searching among the MSS. of the Imperial Record Office, Calcutta, with the happy result of tracing many original documents of great value. No other book on Begam Samru approaches this in fulness and accuracy of information.

It is, besides, a very useful contribution to the true history of the fall of the Mughal empire, which cannot possibly be built up except by a synthesis of many monographs, each exhaustively and critically dealing with its special subject. A beginning in the scientific treatment of this period has been made by Professor K. R. Qanungo in his *History of the Jats*, and Banerji's *Begam Samru* keeps to the same high standard. These examples ought to hearten future workers in the field of Indian history.

JADUNATH SARKAR

AUTHOR'S NOTE

It is not an absolutely new ground that is broken in this work, as more writers than one have touched upon the life of the famous Begam Sombre of Sardhana. But, from the historical point of view, their narratives are of little value, as they are solely based on the accounts left by the European visitors to the Court of the Begam who have recorded, for the most part, bazar gossip and are reliable only so far as they describe things actually seen by them, *viz.*, the condition of the Sardhana principality, and the Begam's character and home life.

On the other hand, my aim has been to produce an authentic and as far as possible complete history of this remarkable lady, and I have therefore made an exhaustive search for the original and contemporary sources of information on the subject. The Mughals, the Marathas, and the British were the chief political Powers in her time, and it was with their history that the life of the princess was closely interwoven. The principal ingredients for the construction of her biography can therefore be gathered only from Persian, Marathi, and English documents of the time. After five or six years' labour in this direction I have been able to unearth much valuable material which is briefly discussed in the bibliography.

Begam Samru deserves an abiding place in our memory as she played no inconspicuous part in the Indian politics of the 18th century. A true estimate of the importance of this character in the history of India, may be formed from the following words of Sir William Sleeman :—

> "For five-and-twenty-years had I been looking forward to the opportunity of seeing this very extraordinary woman, whose history had interested me more than that of any other character in India during my time" (ii. 233).

I take this opportunity of expressing my heartfelt gratitude to Prof. Jadunath Sarkar, M.A., I.E.S. who has not only furnished me with the Persian, French and

Marathi sources on the subject, but has also graced the book with a Foreword. To Mr. A. F. M. Abdul Ali, M.A., Keeper of the Records of the Government of India, are due my thanks for the facilities he has accorded me in making a search among the archives of the Government of India. I am also indebted to my friend, Mr. M. Ray, M.A., Barrister-at-law, for material assistance in the preparation of the MS. for the press.

The likeness of the Begam reproduced here now decorates the hall of Government House, Allahabad, and I hasten to express my best thanks to His Excellency the Governor of the U. P. for his kind permission to take a copy of it. The photograph of the Begam's Delhi palace has been kindly supplied to me by Srijut Jamini Kanta Som, and those of her edifices at Meerut and Sardhana by Sj. Atul Chandra Ganguli, B.A.

BRAJENDRANATH BANERJI

14, PARSI BAGAN,
Calcutta, September, 1925.

CONTENTS

CHAP.		PAGE
I.	An European Adventurer in India	1—13
II.	Early history of Begam Samru ...	14—19
III.	The Begam's Exploits ...	20—29
IV.	The Centre of Delhi Politics ...	30—37
V.	Amour behind the screen ...	38—68
	APPENDIX *A*.—Levassoult's letter to the English	69—71
VI.	Sardhana under British Protection	72—107
	APPENDIX *B*.—Begam to Wellesley	108—109
	APPENDIX *C*.—Edmonstone to the Resident at Delhi	110—113
VII.	Latter days of Begam Samru ...	114—133
VIII.	Begam Samru's Possessions ...	134—158
IX.	Administration and Policy ...	159—172
	APPENDIX *D*.—Adverse criticism of her administration	173—175
X.	Glimpses of the Court of Sardhana	176—187
XI.	History of the Begam's Fortune	188—205
	APPENDIX *E*.—Pension Lists ...	206—208
	APPENDIX *F*.—Funeral Oration ...	209—211
	BIBLIOGRAPHY	212—220
	INDEX	221

ILLUSTRATIONS

1. Begam Samru in old age — *Frontispiece*
   (Now in Allahabad Govt. House)
2. Emperor Shah Alam II — FACING PAGE 9
   (From a contemporary painting)
   General Samru
   (From a miniature in the Victoria Memorial Museum, Calcutta)
3. Genl. George Thomas 19
   Begam Samru's Seal
4. Mahadji Sindhia 21
5. Delhi Palace 153
   St. John's School—Meerut.
6. Sardhana Palace 155
   St. John's College—Sardhana
7. St. Mary's Cathedral Church—Sardhana ... 157
8. Begam's Statue—Sardhana 159
   (By the courtesy of the Arch. Survey of India)

CORRECTIONS

P. 17 footnote line 5 *for* crops *read* corps

,, 146 line 25 ,, 1810 ,, 1809

,, 147 ,, 17 ,, 149 ,, 178

,, 155 footnote line 3 ,, repair ,, repairs

,, 163 head-line *should read* English Admiration for Begam

BEGAM SAMRU IN OLD AGE

Frontispiece]

BEGAM SAMRU

CHAPTER I

AN EUROPEAN ADVENTURER IN INDIA

The latter half of the 18th century was the golden age of European soldiers of fortune in India. When we bear in mind that the Indians of that age were not utterly wanting in valour, military skill, and intellectual keenness, we are apt to wonder how so many ordinary foreign adventurers could attain to the highest power and influence in the camps and Courts of our rulers. India could then boast of generals like Mahadji Sindhia, Parashuram Bhao Patvardhan, Tukoji Holkar, and Haidar Ali, and of statesmen like Mirza Najaf Khan and Nana Fadnavis. On the other hand, the famous European adventurers of the age were not men of outstanding ability or heroic character, though they possessed indefatigable energy, an iron will, and unfailing resourcefulness. De Boigne and

Raymond could lay claim to some military training received in Europe. But Perron was only a runaway sailor, and so were Pedrons, Bourquin and George Thomas. Walter Reinhardt (Samru) and Rene Madec would have been estimated as mediocre soldiers in their homelands. Their private character was stained by unscrupulous selfishness, greed of gold, and lack of fidelity to any master or any noble ideal. How then could such men dominate the political scene in India? The reason will become clear if we contrast Europe and India and remember that the individual, however poor, is still the heir to his *nation's* achievements.

In the 16th century when the Mughal Emperor Akbar adorned the throne of Delhi, Europe and Asia were almost peers in the art of warfare. But thereafter the Europeans, as progressive nations, rapidly improved this art by their zeal and unwearied efforts, while the Indians remained just where they were, content with their antiquated weapons and tactics. During the reign of Akbar and even that of Aurangzib, we find the Europeans in their service in all departments far below the Indians in efficiency and, as such, they could not secure high posts in the army. As an instance, the name of Bernier might be mentioned; this gentleman used to address Danishmand Khan, the minister of Aurangzib, as his *Agha* a term applied to one's master. But in the 18th century the position was inverted. The enterprising and advanced Westerners were the *de facto* masters of the situation, and the sons of the soil were mere puppets in their hands. As for illustration, we might name Gurgin Khan of Nawab Mir Qasim's *darbar*, and Bussy, the Frenchman in the Nizam's Dominions.

That every European was naturally a past master in the art of warfare was an idea which became deeply rooted in the minds of the Indian people in the late 18th century. And the impression was not groundless. Dupleix with a small body of French soldiers and sepoys had successfully stemmed the surging tide of the Karnatak Nawab Anwar-ud-din's mighty host. The English merchants of Bombay with only 1,500 soldiers at their back had the audacity to declare war against the whole Maratha confederacy, and though in an open action the English were repulsed, the admirable behaviour of the British soldiers and the masterly manœuvres of their generals during this campaign and their splendid victories at Gwalior and in Gujrat left an abiding impression on the mind of Sindhia, himself a great general. Ever since then, Sindhia was anxious to train his soldiers on European lines. Following in his footsteps, Holkar and the Peshwa also enlisted English captains for imparting military education to their Indian forces. The rulers of smaller kingdoms, struck by the superior military skill of the foreigners, were eager to engage Europeans as commanders of their armies.

Amongst these adventurers was a German named Walter Reinhardt. Early in life he had enlisted under the French flag and, after spending some time in Southern India, joined the French forces at the settlement of Chandernagar. But after the seizure of Chandernagar by the British (1757), he for a while wandered about in Bengal, and was ultimately engaged by Gurgin Khan, the Armenian general of Mir Qasim, the Nawab of

Bengal, who was then organizing his forces on the European model.

Reinhardt was by temperament a grave, sullen and morose man; and the gloom of his countenance gained for him the nickname of *Sombre* from his friends while he was in the French service. This rather harsh appellation was softened on the Indian tongue into *Samru.** It was not his name only that underwent a change, but his nature and personality also were altered by close contact with Indian life. He "adopted the manners and customs of the country; wore the Mughal dress, and had a zenana. He was versed in the Persian and Moorish tongues, both of which he spoke fluently, and accurately enough."†

Fortune smiled on Samru, and he soon won the heart of his master and became a special favourite with him. But

---

* According to other accounts *Samru* is the corruption of an alias, *Summers*, assumed by him when he enlisted in the British army.

† Major Polier. *Asiatic Annual Register*, 1800, "Mis. Tracts," pp. 31-32.

In his letter, dated 22nd May 1776, Polier writes from Delhi,—"He [Samru] is about 56 years of age, and has an only son about 12." (*Ibid.* p. 32).

the manner in which he discharged the debt of gratitude to the Nawab has cast a slur on his character. Mir Qasim was not a bad man by nature, but, goaded to madness by the repeated wrongs he had received at the hands of the servants of the English East India Company, he determined to emancipate himself from the bondage of the English and prepared for hostilities. Mr. Ellis, the chief of the Factory at Patna, together with other Europeans, who had made an unprovoked attack upon his city of Patna, was captured and ordered to be shot. It was Samru who carried out the execution of these prisoners—numbering 51—at Patna on 5th October 1763. At the battle of Buxar, fought with the English on 23rd October 1764, the Nawabs of Oudh and Bengal met with a decisive reverse. Thereupon Samru, who had raised a body of troops—officered by Europeans—on his own account, roamed about for some time as a free-lance together with his followers, and at last joined the army of Jawahir Singh, the Jat chief of Bharatpur, about April 1765. On the death of Jawahir in 1772, confusion fell upon the kingdom of the Jats. Najaf Khan (Zulfiqar-ud-daula), the premier noble of the Emperor of Delhi, seized this opportunity and proceeded to reduce the Jats. The Jat Rajah Nawal Singh marched from the fort of Deeg with a powerful army, including several regiments of sepoys, trained in European tactics and commanded by Samru and some Frenchmen. The opposing forces met at Barsana and a hard-fought action ensued (October 1773). Here the forces under Samru, though defeated in the end, acquitted themselves with credit.*

Impressed by the military skill displayed by Samru and his French officers, Najaf Khan started negotiations with the object of winning him over from the service of the Jat Rajah. Samru was finally offered Rs. 30,000† a month, his services being considered necessary for occupying and regulating the Agra district, the capital city of which the Khan recovered from

* For the details of Samru's career in the Jat service, Qanungo's *History of the Jats*, i. 80, 195, 210, 232, 265-67.

† In the particulars of the Emperor's expenses for one month, compiled by Md. Elich Khan (1774), we find an item "Samru Feringhy Rs. 30,000." *Calendar of Pers. Correspondence*, iv. 163.

the Jats in the beginning of February 1774. The free-lance realized that the Jat Rajah's service was no longer attractive. He forwarded to the Emperor all the letters he had received from Najaf Khan and begged for a pardon.*

Shah Alam II—a feeble voluptuary—then filled the throne of Delhi. He was a mere puppet in the hands of his *naib-wazir*, Abdul Ahad Khan (Majd-ud-daula), who, out of jealousy for Najaf Khan's growing fame and power, started intriguing against him. With a view to divert Samru from the army of the Amir-ul-umara, Abdul Ahad represented to the Emperor that the Sikhs had become very troublesome and had plundered and burnt Shahdara, almost at the gates of Delhi, and that as a means of punishing them and at the same time preventing Samru from joining other rebels in future, he should be given a pardon and taken into the imperial service. The Emperor approved of the proposal and Samru was sent for. "Samru was presented on 21st May, 1774 and was received very

* *Pers. Correspondence*, iv. 206.

SHAH ALAM II
Emperor of Delhi

GENERAL SAMRU

graciously by His Majesty. A salute was fired on the occasion and every mark of attention shown to him. After presenting *nazar* to the king, Samru said that the enmity between him and the English was such as precluded every possibility of reconciliation. Therefore, if the English or Shuja-ud-daula made any overtures to His Majesty, no notice need be taken. The king then asked him to be easy on that account."*

Samru was ordered to lead an expedition against the Sikhs for recovering the imperial territories usurped by them. Instead of regular pay, he was granted *sanads* for Panipat and Sonipat for his support, and was authorized to possess himself of whatever places he could wrest from Kuchait Singh, the Sikh *faujdar* of Karnal. "Samru had at this time with him 5 pieces of new cannon, a considerable quantity of ammunition, about 1,900 sepoys with a few Europeans and 6 elephants."†

---

* *Pers. Corr.* iv. 195; *Waqa-i-Shah Alam Sani,* MS. *f.* 278.

† *Vol. of Eng. Trans. of Pers. Letters Received* 1774, No. 187, pp. 356-57.

But Najaf Khan, who was bent on continuing his operations against the Jats, could ill afford to spare General Samru with his intimate knowledge of the Jat country and Court. He therefore sent some secret letters containing lucrative offers to the general, who now wrote to Abdul Ahad Khan (August 1774) to the effect that "from the parganas granted to him for the support of his troops he was not able to collect more than Rs. 5,000 from Panipat, Rs. 3,000 from Sambhalka, and a trifling sum from Gharaunda after deducting the necessary charges. The whole collection was not adequate for the payment of the forces, and he had to spend whatever he had of his own. He wrote from 10 to 15 letters requesting the allotment of more places for the support of the troops, but no heed was paid to them. After waiting in vain for a considerable length of time in expectation of receiving assistance, he has determined to look out for a subsistence elsewhere."*

Najaf Khan's repeated victories over the Jats retrieved the prestige of the

---

* *Pers. Correspondence*, iv. 234, also 228.

imperial Government. Samru had grown tired of wandering from Court to Court as a free-lance and now longed for a secure and settled residence.* It was evidently Najaf Khan who finally secured from the Delhi Emperor a *jagir* for his maintenance, and thus the rover became a landed magnate.†

Ever since Samru's flight after the defeat at Buxar, the English had been trying to get him outlawed and driven out of his refuge. But Samru managed to defeat their efforts every time. And in the

---

* Samru was in the service of Najaf Khan as late as June 1777, according to *Vol. of Eng. Trans. of Pers. Letters Written* 1777, No. 74.

† It appears from the following passage in Polier's letter that on the date of his writing—*viz.*, 20th May 1776—Samru was not in possession of this fief: "His party is not very considerable. Three battalions of sepoys and about 200 horse compose it; but he has a good train of artillery, 14 guns well mounted and well served with everything necessary...... He will not take from Najaf Khan any other subsidy for his troops but ready money, which the latter is not very forward to pay. He is actually ten months in arrears with Sombre, and the latter four months in arrears with his own party. If Sombre would accept of a district, which Najaf Khan has more than once offered him, from the rents of which he might get what is sufficient to pay himself his monthly allowance, which is rated at Rs. 65,000, all included, everything would go well with him."—*As. Annual Register*, 1800, p. 31.

end the Emperor of Delhi found his services to be of so much value as to outweigh the risk of English displeasure. Accordingly, he was definitely associated with the imperial Government with a princely grant of lands for his maintenance. This *jagir*, which yielded an annual revenue of six lakhs of Rupees, was situated in the Gangetic Doab and stretched from Aligarh to beyond Muzaffarnagar. Samru selected the village of Sardhana (some 12 miles north-west of Meerut) in its centre for his residence. Such was the origin of what became afterwards famous as the Principality of Sardhana.

But Samru did not live to enjoy his new acquisitions long. He was sent to Agra as its civil and military governor, and died there on 4th May 1778.* "His remains were at first buried in his garden. They were afterwards removed to the

---

* The Portuguese inscription, in raised letters, on his tombstone, in the Roman Catholic Cemetery at Agra, reads :

"Aqui iazo Walter Reinhard morreo aos 4 de Mayo no Anno de 1778."

See *List of Christian Tombs & Monuments*, in charge of the P.W.D., United Provinces, p. 36.

consecrated ground in the Agra church-yard by his widow the Begam" (Sleeman, ii. 273).

The French commandant M. Visage wrote from Gohad on 20th May, 1778,—"Sombre died on the sixth of this month, of a neglected cold. The Nawab [Najaf Khan] has given the same titles that he had to his son and preserved the force. It is Pauli who commands it, pending the time when the younger Reynard [Zafar-yab] will be of an age to command it himself. Sombre died without desiring to confess, nor having put his affairs in any order. His son was sent to his camp [by him] two days before his death" (*Le Nabob Rene Madec*, p. 247).

CHAPTER II

EARLY HISTORY OF BEGAM SAMRU

General Samru, while in the service of the Jat Rajah Jawahir Singh, took part in his master's unsuccessful siege of Delhi in 1765. There a young girl of Arabian extraction was brought to his notice, whose personal attractions and exceptionally fair complexion charmed him. She was united to him "by all the forms considered necessary by persons of her persuasion when married to men of another" (Sleeman, ii. 268). This Muslim girl is known to History as Begam Samru of Sardhana.

Her early life was shrouded in obscurity. We only know that her father was a nobleman named Lutf Ali Khan, who had settled in the town of Kutana, in the Meerut district.* He was married

---

* As for her ancestry I have followed Keegan (*Sardhana*, p. 30) whose version is identical with that of Atkinson (*N.-W. P. Gaz.* ii. 95-96) except that the latter speaks of her as being the daughter, by a concubine, of Asad Khan which may be another name of Lutf Ali Khan or else that of a different person altogether. According to

twice, and our heroine—born in 1750-51* —was his offspring by his second wife. On the death of Lutf Ali, when the Begam was about six years old, her mother was subjected to ill-treatment by her stepson, which drove them out to seek an asylum elsewhere. Both mother and daughter, in the course of their wanderings, "came to Delhi about 1760" (*N.-W.P. Gaz.* ii. 96). The loss of her father, the cruelties of her half-brother, besides many other troubles made her childhood unhappy. The dark clouds, however, soon began to roll away,

---

Sleeman (ii. 267) "she was by birth a Sayyidani, or lineal descendant from Muhammad," while Francklin (*Shah-Aulum,* p. 146) describes her as the "daughter of a Mughal nobleman." Archer (i. 137), Bacon (ii. 35) and Skinner (i. 285) speak of her as belonging originally to a dancing troupe. Bussy was informed (in 1784) by his agents in N. India that she was a Kashmiri.

* According to Beale (*Bio. Dic.* 251), who seems to be very particular about dates, she was aged 88 lunar years when she died on 8 Shawwal 1251 H. (27 Jan. 1836), this age being equivalent to about 85 solar years. This computation places her birth in 1750-51. Dyce Sombre, the adopted son and heir of the Begam, reported her death in a letter, dated 11th July 1836, to the Pope Gregory XVI, wherein her age, at the time of death, is given as 85—evidently solar years. Captain Francklin, the biographer of Geo. Thomas who had served the Begam for some time, when describing the events of 1796, mentions her age as being then about 45, which would place her birth in 1751.

and on the dawning of her youth, bathed in the glamour of her radiant beauty, she came across the path of the general who, as was to be expected, became at once a willing victim to her charms, and the girl passed into the harem of Samru Sahib as his partner in life.

Begam Samru's uncommon beauty and intelligence won the heart of that stern military adventurer, so much so that he now thought more of a life of ease and pleasure than one of campaigning. The Begam made the most of this opportunity. She cleverly contrived to take away from the hands of her lord the actual exercise of all his powers. But this peaceful life he was not destined to enjoy long, as death overtook him in 1778.

There was no issue of their marriage, but Samru had a son by another Muhammadan wife. This son of Samru "got from the Emperor the title of Zafar-yab Khan, at the request of the Begam, his step-mother; but he was a man of weak intellect, and so little thought of that he was not recognized even as the nominal chief on the death of his father. The Begam, therefore, was requested to take command of Samru's forces by all the Europeans and natives that composed it, as the only possible mode of keeping them together. She consented, and was regularly installed in the charge by the Emperor Shah Alam" (Sleeman, ii. 268, 273). She thus attained the dignity and power of an independent ruling princess with an army of her own.

The confidence thus reposed in her by the Emperor was not misplaced. Her soul was heroic, and the battle-field had no terror for her, as she had become accustomed to it by accompanying her husband in several of his campaigns. When she first took command of the army, her chief military officer was a German named Pauli.*

* "The late Mr. Sombre's corps is supposed to be 4,000 strong with 82 European [officers]. The troops of the widow of Sombre are in great misery. This woman, named Paragauna (*sic.* Farzana ?) Begam, residing at Akbarabad near Agra, is at the head of her late husband's crops. Pauli, who used to command it, had awkwardly mixed in intrigues and as a result had been decapitated [by Md. Beg Hamadani, in 1782]. Since then M. Marchand commands it. Believing that Sombre's widow (a native of Kashmir) is very rich, M. Montigny wanted to marry her and command her troops. But learning of Pauli's murder and the confiscation of the widow's property, he gave the idea up." [Pondicherry Records. Bussy to Marshal de Castries, 3 March, 1784].

2

Three years after the death of her husband she, along with her stepson Zafar-yab—doubtless under the persuasion of her European officers—was baptized as a Christian at Agra on 7th May, 1781 by Fr. Gregorio, a Roman Catholic priest, when she was christened *Joanna* and her stepson *Louis Balthazar Reinhardt* (Sleeman, ii. 273).

Some five years later a very extraordinary man entered her service. He was the celebrated adventurer George Thomas, a native of Tipperary in Ireland. Thomas came to India in 1781-82 as a quartermaster—or as is affirmed by some, as a common sailor in a British man-of-war—and deserting his ship took service for a few years among the Polygars of the Karnatak. Spurred on by ambition he travelled overland to Delhi about 1787, where he received a commission under Begam Samru. She with her characteristic judgment and discrimination soon advanced Thomas to the supreme command of her army.

Thomas was a man of great ability and "in various and successive actions against the Sikhs and others of the

GENL. GEORGE THOMAS

BEGAM SAMRU'S SEAL

Begam's enemies, he, by his courage and perseverance, rendered her authority respectable. By these successes, he obtained a considerable influence over the mind of his mistress, and was for some time, her chief adviser and counsellor" (*Thomas*, pp. 2-3). The Sardhana brigade, drilled in European fashion, became formidable under the leadership of Thomas, and the Princess of Sardhana was now looked upon with dread by her neighbours.

CHAPTER III

THE BEGAM'S EXPLOITS

In those troubled times, when Hindustan was in a state of transition, chaos and disruption reigned everywhere. The Maratha Power was in the ascendant, and Mahadji Sindhia as vicegerent of the Emperor of Delhi virtually ruled Northern India. Revolt against the imperial authority became the order of the day. Rajah Pratap Singh of Jainagar (Jaipur) withheld the customary tribute to the Court and, rallying the Rajput magnates round him, unfurled the banner of independence. To subdue him Mahadji himself marched with a large force. There was no dearth of treachery even in his own camp, and the lure of gold enticed away many a dissatisfied Mughal noble to the ranks of the enemy. In the battle that ensued Mahadji was defeated and, smarting under this humiliation, he retreated to Gwalior, to wait for reinforcements from the Deccan. Shah Nizam-ud-din, the deputy of Sindhia, hearing the

MAHADJI SINDHIA

disheartening news of his master's reverse and retreat towards the Deccan, put the fort and city of Delhi into the best possible state of defence as a precautionary measure.

Towards the latter part of 1787 a storm was brewing in the very heart of the capital. Ghulam Qadir, the son of the old Ruhela rebel Zabita Khan, was then the ruler of Saharanpur. Taking advantage of the confusion prevailing at the time, he prepared for carrying out his ambitious schemes and appeared with an army on the eastern bank of the Jamuna opposite the citadel. Qadir was confident of success, as he had attached to his interests a man commanding the greatest influence over the mind and Court of the Emperor. This was Manzur Ali, the treacherous *nazir*, who faithlessly joined in the intrigues of the rebel.

Shah Nizam-ud-din, however, underrated the strength of the Ruhela chief. He sent out a small force across the river to deliver an immediate attack on the enemy's camp, which was repulsed with considerable loss. Shah Nizam-ud-din, sorely disappointed at this defeat and having by this time received intelligence of the treacherous designs of the *nazir*, fled for safety to the fort of Ballamgarh, 22 miles south of Delhi.

With the flight of Sindhia's deputy, the capital stood entirely undefended and the Emperor was in a helpless state. Ghulam Qadir now crossed the river and entered the royal chamber without the least obstruction and demanded from the Emperor the office of the *Amir-ul-umara* or Premier Noble, then held by Sindhia. The helpless Shah Alam II had to agree.

Begam Samru, hearing of the ignominious plight of her sovereign, resolved to advance with all her forces in order to restore him to his legitimate position. "In the war against Pratap Singh, Begam Samru with her force was stationed at Panipat on the frontier; and committing so important a trust to her charge was a sufficient proof of the idea the Maratha chief had conceived of her capacity. Her conduct now evinced that that confidence had not been misplaced, and her spirited exertions in defence of the king's authority acquired deserved applause in the breasts of all" (*Shah-Aulum*, p. 148).

Ghulam Qadir was not ignorant of the Begam's influence at the imperial Court, and he was much alarmed when he learnt that she was coming in person to liberate the Emperor. "Being frightened at her hostile attitude, the artful Ruhela one day went to her camp, situated outside the Delhi fort, accompanied by only two servants. He called her his sister, and tried to make friends with her. She, however, knew his reputation for cunning and deception, and therefore outwardly promised to join him with her troops—four *paltans* of sepoys trained for battle with 85 guns—after he had crossed over to the other side of the Jamuna. Falling into her trap he did so, when she guarded the ferry by means of one *paltan* of her sepoys and some guns to prevent his return! Thus the Emperor was saved" (*Ibratnama*, iii. 26-7).

Had she consented to the ignoble proposal of the powerful miscreant, she might have made herself the mistress of an immense fortune. The Begam, however, rose to the occasion and "rejected all his solicitations; and to give proof of her resolution to maintain the king's authority, she with her whole force repaired to the palace, and declared her intention of sacrificing her life in his Majesty's cause" (*Shah-Aulum*, p. 148). Her loyal devotion in scorn of riches and power stands out in signal contrast to the black treachery of the Ruhela rebel.

"Baffled in his attempts to acquire the Begam's support, Qadir was inflamed with savage fury. Going to his camp on the opposite bank of the Jamuna, he thence despatched a messenger to the Court, demanding in terms most peremptory, the immediate removal of Samru's wife, adding, that in the event of non-compliance he should proceed to hostilities. His message having been treated with the contempt it deserved, Ghulam Qadir commenced a heavy cannonade upon the royal palace. This was answered from some artillery in the fort, from the guns attached to the Mughal battalions in his Majesty's service, and from a battery which had been erected with great expedition by Begam Samru. . . . . During this disgraceful scene, intelligence arrived that Prince Mirza Jawan Bakht, accompanied by a large army, was on his march to the capital. Of this event the *nazir* conveyed private information to Ghulam Qadir, and foreseeing that the prince's arrival would disconcert his perfidious schemes, he strongly recommended the Ruhela to make immediate overtures for a pacification..............Qadir, therefore, having signified to his Majesty his sincere contrition for the late insult, presented a handsome *peshkash* in ready money, and, moreover, promised to restore all the royal lands in the Doab which he had lately usurped*..............Urged by the repeated solicitations of the *nazir*, the Emperor acquiesced in the proposal. The terms being settled, an honorary dress was despatched over the river to Ghulam Qadir Khan, who immediately after receiving it, struck his camp, and returned to Saharanpur" (*Shah-Aulum*, pp. 148-150).

The disorder in the capital offered an opportunity to some of the zamindars who, from their remote situation, could

* It is stated in the *Ibratnama* (*f.* 63) that the Emperor had granted Rs. 1,000 daily to Begam Samru, because her *jagirs* were in Ghulam Qadir's possession. This temporary usurpation of the Begam's *jagirs* must have taken place during the close of 1787.

safely withhold the payment of the revenue and refuse allegiance to the imperial Court. Najaf Quli Khan was one of these refractory men. On 8th January, 1788, the Emperor Shah Alam proceeded with his forces to subdue this chief, whose stronghold was the fort of Gokulgarh* in Rajputana. Begam Samru accompanied the expedition with her contingent, "composed of three disciplined battalions of sepoys, which had belonged to the late Samru, and were then commanded by his Begam in person, and furnished with a respectable artillery served by European cannoneers" (*Shah-Aulum*, p. 162). The imperialists sat down before the walls of Gokulgarh, but owing to certain of their officers being negligent on the watch, they were surprised and thrown into utter confusion by a sortie of the garrison at early dawn. The besieging line gave way. The royal tent being within cannon shot, the Emperor was exposed to the greatest

---

* When the Emperor went with the princes to invade Rajputana, a night-attack was made on his camp near Rewari, which is 49 miles south-west of Delhi, by Ghulam Husain, a slave of Najaf Quli, from the fort and by Major Neir [?] with a detachment from the army of Najaf Quli (*Ibratnama*, iii. 126).

personal risk. At this juncture, when the Emperor's life was in danger, it was the gallantry of Begam Samru that saved him.

"That spirited woman was encamped to the right of the line; her force remained entire, unaffected by the general panic and stood ready in dressed ranks. On perceiving the extreme confusion that reigned throughout the line, she bravely resolved, by a personal effort, to prevent the king's disgrace; she sent a respectful message to his Majesty, desiring him to repair to her quarters, and assured him of her determined resolution to punish the rebel, or perish in the attempt. At the same time, she, on the field, wrote a short note, which she despatched to Najaf Quli Khan, upbraiding him with his ingratitude towards the king, and threatening him with immediate and exemplary chastisement. The gallant lady then getting into her palanquin, placed herself at the head of 100 of her own sepoys, accompanied by a six-pounder, commanded by a European officer [George Thomas, see *Thomas*, 3*n*]. With this detachment she proceeded to the spot occupied by Mansur Khan, and advancing upon the rebel with much spirit, she commanded her palanquin to be set down, and ordered her artillery to charge with grape-shot; a well-directed fire from the gun, assisted by vollies of small arms from the sepoys, soon had the desired effect.... Order being once more restored, the king directed his tents to be pitched, which done, he bethought of bestowing a suitable reward to the gallant female who had preserved him from imminent destruction. Having sent for her to the *darbar*, in the warmest terms he praised her gallantry, and thanked her for the service she had that day rendered him; he clothed her in a magnificent vest, and, in addition to her former titles,* honoured her with the appellation of 'his most beloved daughter.' It was, indeed, by all acknowledged, that the intrepidity manifested by the Begam on so trying an occasion, merited the most honourable reward; to her courage and resolution was owing, not only the safety of the army, but

* She had on a former occasion been given by the Emperor the title of *Zeb-un-nisa* or 'the Ornament of the Sex.'

her sovereign's life" (*Shah-Aulum*, pp. 164-166).

Dispirited at his defeat,* Najaf Quli now approached the Begam, who had great influence at the Court of Delhi, begging her to plead for his pardon with the Emperor. She consented to intercede on his behalf and the Emperor "to comply with her request" (*Ibratnama*, iii. 127) fully pardoned Najaf Quli Khan.†

---

* According to Atkinson (*N.-W. P. Gaz.* ii. 99) the Emperor Shah Alam on this occasion conferred on her a valuable estate called pargana Badshapur-Jharsa in *jagir* situated on the west of the Jamuna. Probably this is the property referred to by Francklin (*Shah-Aulum*, p. 148) and, following him, by Skinner (*Memr.*, p. 285), when they remark that Sindhia, when arrived at supreme power, added to the extent of her possessions by a grant of some other lands south-west of the Jamuna.

It, however, appears from a perusal of the *Privy Council Judgments* (1872 May) that the estate was bestowed as a jagir (which may be a mere estate for life) upon Zafar-yab Khan, the stepson of the Begam, by Shah Alam sometime in the 30th year of his reign which corresponded to 1787-88. But the Begam had in some way usurped his interest and was found in the enjoyment of it during her life.

† Ghulam Qadir's temporary usurpation :—*Ibratnama*, iii. 26-27; *Shah-Aulum*, pp. 145, 148-50.

Najaf Quli's night-attack :—*Ibratnama*, iii. 126-27; *Shah-Aulum*, pp. 162-66.

CHAPTER IV

THE CENTRE OF DELHI POLITICS

The defeat of Mahadji Sindhia at Ajmir in the latter half of 1787 by the Rajput confederacy under the Jaipur Rajah eclipsed the Maratha influence over the throne of Delhi for a time, as Sindhia had no agent capable of maintaining his hold on the Emperor during his own absence.* The imbecile monarch was steeped in pleasure and indolence, and the administration virtually rested with his faithless *nazir*, Manzur Ali, whom the infatuated Emperor prized as his most devoted servant. The eldest son of the Emperor, Mirza Jawan Bakht Jahandar

* Ambaji Dhara Rao—sent by Sindhia to reinforce the *subahdar* of Ajmir—is defeated by the Rajputs. He goes to Delhi and meets the Emperor, seeking his aid. Manzur Ali Khan (the *nazir*) turns the Emperor's mind against them, and the Mughal *sawars* crowd at the palace door, asking for permission to loot Ambaji and other Marathas. But Zeb-un-nisa (Begam Samru), who is in the environs of Delhi, and with whom Ambaji has abjectly sought refuge, protects them with her European-style-disciplined troops. She sends a party of her troops and extricates him from this danger (Nov. 1787).—*Ibratnama,* iii. 53.

Shah, who had been living in retirement far away from the capital, received intelligence of Ghulam Qadir's late conduct and the disgraceful state of things at Court. He now resolved to proceed to Delhi, wishing to conciliate the Mughal nobility and, with their assistance, to establish order and tranquillity at the capital, and thereby seek to restore the lost glory of the Mughal empire.

Begam Samru was an important figure in Delhi politics at this time, and therefore her friendly counsels and help were considered invaluable by the prince. He now sent from his camp at Faridabad his constant companion Faqir Khair-ud-din Muhammad, as his minister plenipotentiary to negotiate with her.

Khair-ud-din reached Delhi by *dâk* in six hours and went to the camp of Begam Samru outside the city. On hearing of his approach she held a splendid *darbar*, bidding her French, Armenian, Portuguese and other captains to be present, while she herself sat behind a screen. After tedious formalities Khair-ud-din opened the object of his embassy. The Begam asked him, 'Does your prince possess any manly and heroic qualities?' He answered, 'The day is near when you yourself will test it personally in an interview with him. I find his external appearance to be as it ought to be.'

"She said, 'What joking is this? What I meant to ask was, whether he possessed the capacity to play the sword and win kingdoms, or only a passion for playing on the drum and tabor.'

"He replied, 'If he were not such a hero and man of enterprise, he would not have turned to thee. If he were a coward and pleasure-seeker he would not have asked for thee.'

"She then said, 'I have heard that he is capricious and constantly changing his mind.' [Then she narrated a well-known Persian anecdote.]

"She agreed that when next day the prince would enter the palace to interview his father, she would send a *paltan* of sepoys inside the Delhi fort and, thus strengthened, the prince would demand of the Emperor that he should be appointed regent. Thereafter the prince would remain in the fort and manage the affairs of State" (*Ibratnama*, iii. 62-63).

The return of the heir-apparent after a long absence and especially in such a time of distress, was at first looked upon with joy by the Emperor who promised to invest him with the management of affairs. But in order to effect the total overthrow of the Maratha usurpation and to establish order and peace, it was necessary to place the imperial treasury and army under the direct control of the prince.

But alas! the fall of the Mughal Emperor was not to be averted. He was virtually a puppet in the hands of his *nazir*, Manzur Ali, who, envious of the prince's authority, instilled into his weak old master's mind an ugly suspicion about his heir's loyalty, and thus succeeded in ruining the cause of the prince—materially assisted though he was by Begam Samru. At last the prince retired from the Court in despair, to die at Benares in May 1788, as a heart-broken noble youth.*

The retirement of the prince from the scene and the absence of Begam Samru from Delhi put the capital in a defenceless

* For a detailed account of the prince's fruitless attempt, see *Ibratnama*, iii. 58-59, 62-63; *Shah-Aulum*, pp. 149-157.

state. Ghulam Qadir now thought it fit to strike a decisive blow. He easily gained access to the palace with the connivance of his friend, nazir Manzur Ali, and filled it with his own troops. The rebel now proceeded to the Emperor and demanded his hidden treasures. In vain did Shah Alam plead the emptiness of the imperial coffers, but it only enraged Qadir, who dethroned him and placed Bidar Bakht, a son of the late Emperor Ahmad Shah, on the throne. Shah Alam and the princes were held prisoners. "Qadir went to Shah Alam, and said, 'Find me some gold, or I will send you to join the dead.' Shah Alam reviled and reproached him, saying, 'I am in your power, cut off my head, for it is better to die than to live like this.' Ghulam Qadir sprang up, and threw himself upon the Emperor's bosom, Qandahari Khan and Purdil Khan seized his hands, two of their companions held his feet; Qandahari Khan tore out one of his eyes, and that blood-thirsty ruffian tore out the other with his own hands, amid the wailings of the Emperor........Then he called for a painter, and said 'Paint my likeness at once, sitting knife in hand, upon the breast of Shah Alam, digging out his eyes' " [10th August, 1788. *Ibratnama* in Elliot, viii. 248-49]. Now the ladies' apartments were ransacked. "Neither Nadir Shah, Ahmad Shah Durrani, nor the Bhao, had ever dreamed of plundering the ladies of the harem; but now all valuables, the accumulations of fifty or sixty years, were brought out" (*Ibid.* p. 250). "Ghulam Qadir heard of the beauty of the daughters of Mirza Haika and Mirza Jaika, and when he was sitting in the Moti Mahal in the evening, he ordered these unhappy ladies to be placed before him without veils or curtains. He was pleased with their beauty, showed them to his boon companions, and acted indecently to every one of them" (*Ibid.* p. 252).

But the day of agony at last came to a close. Sindhia had entered the Doab again with a formidable army. When these tragic events came to his knowledge, he at once sent his general Ranah Khan to expel the traitor and to liberate the Emperor. Ghulam Qadir now found his situation in the imperial palace untenable and prepared for flight; he collected all his plunder, left the fort, and retreated to Meerut along with his puppet Emperor and the infamous *nazir*.

The Maratha general hastened to the palace, released the dethroned Shah Alam, caused him to be proclaimed again as Emperor of Delhi, and made the requisite arrangements for his comfort. He then took up the pursuit of the rebel, who was eventually captured alive.

Ghulam Qadir was placed in an iron cage, with a chain put upon "his legs, a collar on his neck, and conveyed in a bullock carriage to Sindhia, guarded by two regiments of sepoys and a thousand horse.........Under the orders of Sindhia, the ears of Ghulam Qadir were cut off and hung round his neck, his face was blackened, and he was carried round the camp and city. Next day his nose and upper lip were cut off, and he was again paraded. On the third day he was thrown upon the ground, his eyes were torn out, and he was once more carried round. After that his hands were cut off, then his feet, and last of all his head.........Maharajah Sindhia sent the ears and eye-balls to the Emperor Shah Alam" (*Ibratnama* in Elliot, viii.

254). The wicked *nazir* also atoned for his crimes by being trodden to death under the feet of an elephant.

CHAPTER V

AMOUR BEHIND THE SCREEN

Following the practice of many other Indian chieftains of the time, Begam Samru entrusted the command of her armies to European officers. In 1790 her highest general was an Irishman named George Thomas, who was also her chief adviser and counsellor. About this time a young Frenchman named Levassoult entered her service. He soon rose in the estimation of his mistress by reason of his personal charms as well as his military prowess. Unfortunately for Thomas, Levassoult gradually supplanted him in the good graces of the Begam. Her partiality for Levassoult exciting much animosity and heart-burning between the two rival commanders, Thomas in disgust quitted the Begam's service about 1792.* (*Thomas*, p. 3).

---

*The circumstances attending the resignation of George Thomas are related differently :

According to a letter, dated April 1794, from the Maratha envoy resident at Delhi, addressed to his master at Puna,

His rival having departed, Levassoult became the master of the situation at Sardhana. With the increase of his power his ambition grew higher, and he resolved to consolidate his position by marrying the Begam. The Begam in spite of her forty winters still retained much of her beauty and youth, and was not at all averse to the attentions of the ardent Frenchman. She consented to marry Levassoult but wished to keep the affair secret, as she feared that she might lower herself in public esteem and compromise her position as Sombre's heiress by openly marrying one beneath her rank. The marriage was secretly performed

---

"the Begam was forced to drive out George Thomas from her territory on account of his loose morals—*batay-baji*" (*Dilli-yathil*, ii. 105).

But a Lucknow correspondent in his "authentic account of Geo. Thomas" published in the columns of the *Asiatic Annual Register* (1802,'Characters,' pp. 55-56) assigns a different cause. Thomas wanted to curtail the number of Frenchmen in the service of the Begam as her expenses exceeded her income. This enraged the Frenchmen and, while Thomas was away on a campaign against the Sikhs, they induced their mistress to believe that he was scheming to rob her of her possessions and that was why he had wished for their dismissal. She vented her displeasure on Thomas's wife. He immediately returned, rescued his wife, and left her service.

in 1793* by the Rev. Fr. Gregorio, a Carmelite monk, with Roman Catholic rites, and was witnessed only by two brother officers and countrymen of the bridegroom—Bernier and Saleur. At the time of her marriage the Begam "added the name of *Nobilis*" to her Christian name of Joanna. (*N.-W. P. Gaz.* ii. 106*n*).

Little did the Begam imagine how disastrous this marriage would prove to her. She had been carried away by the impulse of the moment and had not stopped to consider how it would affect Levassoult's future conduct. Compared with the other military officers in her service, Levassoult was by far the most educated and polished. But he had one great failing, namely arrogance, which increased with his power. Even before his marriage he was reserved and did not mix freely with the other officers, whom

*Sleeman observes that "as the best chance of securing his ascendancy against such a rival, Levassoult proposed marriage to the Begam, and was accepted. She was married to him in 1793. Geo. Thomas left her service *in consequence*, in 1793." But Francklin, the biographer of Thomas, was clearly under the impression that Thomas had thrown up the Begam's command about 1792—prior to her marriage. (*Thomas*, pp. 3, 31).

he considered his inferiors in birth and culture. The Begam, on the other hand, always treated them as friends, because she knew full well that her fortune depended on keeping her army contented and, to gain this end, she used to invite her principal officers to dine with her. After the marriage Levassoult objected to this practice as humiliating to her position and refused to receive them at the table. The officers deeply resented this insult from one whom they considered their equal, and wondered why the Begam permitted such conduct. Levassoult was also indiscreetly open in his relations with the Begam, and therefore the public knowing nothing of the marriage naturally looked upon him as her paramour. These matters did not escape the vigilant lady's notice, and she apprehended that her husband's conduct would lead to a disaster at no distant date. She tried her best to make him realize the gravity of the situation and mend his ways, but all her persuasions fell on deaf ears.

Meanwhile, Thomas had obtained a command in the service of the Maratha chief Appa Khande Rao (Khande Rao Hari), and having recruited a fresh army proceeded in 1793 to the parganas in the Mewat district (s.-w. of Delhi) entrusted to his care; "on the way he retaliated upon the Begam, whom he now considered his bitter enemy, [by] laying under contribution that part of her country which came within his route" (*Thomas*, 14-15; *Dilli-yethil Rajkaranen*, ii. 105). Under his able generalship Appa's army gained several brilliant victories, and his power and territory grew apace. On the death of Mahadji Sindhia,* 12th February 1794, the stability of the Maratha Power in Northern India was shaken, and Appa tried to avail himself of this opportunity to usurp the supreme authority at Delhi. The Prince-Regent Mirza Akbar, acting on behalf of the blind and infirm Emperor Shah Alam II, apprehended a possible rising and "wrote to the Begam and some of the nobles, 'Recruit an army, and I will provide and send you the necessary funds.'

*Mahadji Sindhia was succeeded by his grand-nephew, Daulat Rao Sindhia, who was scarcely 15 years old at the time.

Rennel Sahib [elsewhere *Jernel*=general] left Delhi with this letter for the residence of the Begam at Sardhana." (Letter dated 30-3-1794, *Dilli-yethil*, ii. 100).

It appears that the Emperor's son considered Appa too formidable an enemy, and intended to seek the help of the British; but not daring to do so openly lest other Maratha chiefs should resent the British intervention and therefore side with Appa, decided to secretly approach the Governor-General for help so as not to compromise his position in the event of a refusal. Prince Akbar did not want to disclose to the British the fact that their help was really solicited on behalf of the Emperor himself. Begam Samru, being on friendly terms with them, and a feud existing between her and Thomas, the Begam's party wanted to make it appear that Appa was trying to ruin her at the instigation of Thomas.

The matter demanding the strictest secrecy, the Begam decided to send one of her most trustworthy counsellors to carry on negotiations verbally and the choice fell upon Padre Gregorio—the almoner of her party—who being a European, would.

it was thought, be better received at the Governor-General's Court.* In a letter, addressed to the Governor-General on 16th June 1794 (17 Ziqada 1208 H.), the Begam wrote:

> "Although by the favour of God I here find no deficiency in anything, everything being present and at hand, and that in this country connected with sardars of renown I have by proper attention met with favour and attained a degree of authority and respectability, yet at this time I find myself oppressed by the haughty demeanour of a sardar of renown in this quarter and I hope for your exertions and kindness in the manner expressed in your obliging letter. . . Fr. Gregori, who will have the honour to pay his respects to you, will communicate all particulars."†

The Rev. Father, after a stay of three months in Calcutta, left for Sardhana in September 1794, disappointed in the

---

*The Begam addressed the Governor-General on the subject of Fr. Gregorio's mission in her letter, written in English on 6 March 1794 (*Pol. Procdgs.* 30-6-1794, No. 24) and in a Persian letter—received by the Governor-General on 30th June 1794 (*Vol. of Eng. Trans. of Pers. Letters Received* 1794, No. 360). These letters do not discuss the object of the mission and are merely letters of introduction.

†*Original Letter* No. 109; *Vol. of Eng. Trans. of Pers. Letters Received*, 5-7-1794, No. 367.

object of his mission, as the Governor-General was evidently unwilling to interfere in the matter:

> "The receipt of your letter [recd. 30 June] which with the presents your friendship induced you to send was delivered to me by the Fr. Gregori, afforded me great pleasure. His arrival and the accounts I have received from him of your attachment to this Government have been highly satisfactory. In the course of several interviews I have had with him I have been made acquainted with the points entrusted to his disclosure and in the answers I have given to them, I have not been unmindful of the friendship you bear towards this Government whilst they have been necessarily guided by those maxims and established principles which form the basis of its measures in its intercourse with the chiefs of Hindustan. The Father will verbally detail them to you. He now takes his leave."*

In the meantime, "jealous of the ascendancy Mr. Thomas had acquired, the Begam and the Maratha governor of Delhi had sent a force to watch Thomas's movements" (*Thomas*, 19), who knew

* Letter, dated 9 September 1794, from the Governor-General to Zeb-un-nisa Begam.—*Vol. of Eng. Trans. of Pers. Letters Written*, 1794, No. 260.

nothing of the Begam's plan. On the failure of Fr. Gregorio's mission the Begam decided to attack Appa's forces. The subsequent events are graphically described by Thomas in his *Military Memoirs*, though of course he says nothing of the diplomatic moves leading up to the attack, of which he was totally ignorant.

"Begam Samru, in whose service Mr. Thomas had formerly been employed, was now trying every means in her power to effect his ruin. She had even gone so far as to bribe the Maratha officers to advise his dismission; and a body of Marathas having joined her army, she marched from Sardhana her capital, and encamped about 17 *kos* south-east of Jhujjar. This conduct in the Begam Mr. Thomas attributed to the influence of the officers in her service, and more particularly to that of Levasso, who not only commanded her troops, but had lately received her hand in marriage. On every occasion, he was the declared, and inveterate, enemy of Mr. Thomas; and had by his influence, wrought in the Begam her present determination.

"In the Begam's army it was publicly asserted, that their present destination was against Mr. Thomas, her force, consisting of 4 battalions of infantry, 20 pieces of artillery, and about 400 cavalry, was commanded by officers of tried and acknowledged abilities: Mr. Thomas, having recalled the battalion that had been detached, had now a regiment consisting of 2,000 men, 10 pieces of artillery, 500 irregulars and 200 cavalry.

"The dissensions however that arose among the Begam's officers, not only induced her to relinquish her intention of attacking Mr. Thomas; but ended in her imprisonment, and the total subversion of her authority. The cause of these dissensions must now be traced to its source.

"Levasso who had the chief command of the Begam's army was jealous of the authority of Legois. . . . He had been many years in habits of intimacy and friendship with Mr. Thomas, and on the present occasion, had strenuously dissuaded the Begam from the proposed hostilities. This conduct, having given umbrage to Levasso, he by his influence with the Begam, procured Legois' degradation; and to render his disgrace the more mortifying, his place was given to a junior officer.

"A conduct so inconsistent and unjust, disgusted the soldiers, who for many years, had been commanded by Legois, with whom also they had often fought and conquered. They remonstrated, but in vain, against the measure; finding there was no hope of altering the Begam's resolution, they suddenly broke out into open mutiny" (*Thomas*, pp. 31-33).

The Begam was therefore obliged to relinquish her intention of attacking Thomas, and returned to Sardhana in hot haste. But her officers and soldiers generally grew more and more insolent, and finally refused to be commanded by an arrogant upstart. The very soldiers, who were her strength and support and upon whose valour and devotion she entirely depended for her safety, were now her and her husband's enemies. Their insolence, their secret councils, their suspicious movements, made her nervous. Sardhana was indeed next to her heart, and she felt disconsolate at the thought of parting with it. But she was convinced that her stay at Sardhana was nót safe, and that whatever might be in store for her, it would be impossible to save her lover from the hands of the infuriated soldiery.

The rebels now "invited Zafar-yab Khan, the son of the late Samru, by a former wife, who then resided at Delhi to become their commander. In return, they promised to seat him on the *masnad*. For this purpose, a deputation of the army, in spite of all the exertions of the Begam, repaired to Delhi, and solemnly tendered him the command" (*Thomas*, p. 33).

At the first intelligence of their conspiracy the Begam prepared for flight with her husband. Under her direction, Levassoult wrote a letter sometime in March, 1795 to Lt.-Col. J. M'Gowan who at that time commanded the British advanced post at Anupshahr on the Ganges, 73 miles s.-e. of Delhi. "He proposed that the Colonel should receive them in his cantonments, and assist them in their journey thence to Farrukhabad, where they wished in future to reside, free from the cares and anxieties of such a charge. The Colonel had some scruples, under the impression that he might be censured for aiding in the flight of a public officer of the Emperor" (Sleeman, ii. 279).

But the situation was growing worse and delay would result in serious consequences. On the very day Levassoult received the Colonel's reply (2nd April 1795), he wrote a second letter in conformity with the desire and direction of the Begam:

> " . . . . Maratha amity cannot be hurt by the removal of the Begam into British possessions. . . . She is absolutely fatigued by the duties and cares of the military possession which has been the object of her attendance for a space of eighteen years. She resorts at your friendship, because she cannot by any way whatsoever make her intention known either to the Government to which she is subordinate, or to her own soldiers, without exposing herself to many dangers" (*Refutation*, pp. 443-45).

At the same time the Begam herself addressed the following letter to Sir John Shore which reached the Governor-General's office on 22nd April 1795:

> "From the goodness you were pleased to manifest with respect to me I am confident that my present wish will through your kindness

meet with a favourable reception. The object I had, in sending the Padre was this, that being worn out and oppressed by years and by worldly care I may be permitted to reside either in Bengal or Bihar wherever the gentlemen of the Council may think proper to direct, where I shall not fail to maintain due obedience to their orders but shall on all occasions [act] in strict conformity to their wishes. The Padre, however, forgot this and has returned without success in the object of his going. I now take the liberty to transmit an *arzi* to the address of the gentlemen of the Council with this letter to yours."*

It is hard to believe that the Father, after a three months' stay in Calcutta,

---

* *Vol. of Eng. Trans. of Pers. Letters Received*, 23-4-1795, No. 172.

The *arzi* (recd. on 22 April, 1795) reads as follows:

"I am desirous of living under the protection of the English Government and of residing in some assigned place in Bengal or Bihar. I will act with the strictest conformity to the orders of the gentlemen of the Council and will demean myself as a subject. My life has hitherto been a scene of difficulties and distress: it is now verging towards the close and through age I am unable to support these difficulties any longer, hence I wish to retire and to pass the remainder of my life under the mild protection of the English Government. I ever beseech of God to prosper the English Government and to extend its protection which is my only prospect of support" (*Pol. Procdgs.* 29-5-1795, No. 37).

actually forgot the principal object of his mission. But in the meantime, matters seem to have assumed a serious aspect so that the Begam was anxious to leave Sardhana secretly.

The members of the Calcutta Council considered her petition favourably and passed the following resolution:

> "Agreed that the Governor-General be requested to inform the widow of the late Sombre in answer to her letter, that she is at liberty to reside with her family and personal attendants at Patna, if she thinks proper, excluding from the permission any troops or military whatever" (*Pol. Procdgs.* 29-5-1795, No. 37).

Receiving no reply to her *arzi* the Begam again wrote to Sir John Shore on 6th May 1795:

> "It is long since I have been favoured with letters containing good accounts of your health, be the cause favourable. The attentions you have bestowed on me are indescribable. . . . I have despatched by Mr. Levassoult a letter written in the European character dictated by me and dated *6th May 1795*. Be assured of this and rely on the truth of its contents."*

**Vol. of Eng. Trans. of Pers. Letters Received*, 10-6-1795, No. 219. The date of the letter, which reached the Governor-General's office on 10th June 1795, is given on the envelope, attached to the original letter (No. 147), as 16 Shawwal, year 37th of Shah Alam's reign [1209 H.] =6 May 1795.

It is difficult to say whether the decision of the Calcutta Council was actually conveyed to the Begam by the Governor-General, as I have come across no such statement in the Imperial Record Office, Calcutta.*

---

* From a perusal of Sleeman's account (ii. 279-80) it seems that the Begam obtained the necessary authority from Daulat Rao Sindhia and the Governor-General and completed all arrangements for her departure:

"He now addressed the Governor-General of India, Sir John Shore himself, [in] April 1795, who requested Major Palmer, our accredited agent with Sindhia, who was then encamped near Delhi, and holding the seals of prime-minister of the empire, to interpose his good offices in favour of the Begam and her husband. Sindhia demanded 12 lakhs of Rupees as the price of the privilege she solicited [namely] to retire; and the Begam, in her turn, demanded over and above the privilege of resigning the command into his hands, the sum of 4 lakhs of Rupees as the price of the arms and accoutrements which had been provided at her own cost and that of her late husband. It was at last settled that she should resign the command, and set out secretly with her husband; and that Sindhia should confer the command of her troops upon one of his own officers, who would pay the son of Sombre Rs. 2,000 a month for life. Levassoult was to be received into our territories, treated as a prisoner of war upon parole, and permitted to reside with his wife at the French settlement of Chandernagar. His last letter to Sir John Shore is dated the 30th April, 1795. His last letters describing this final arrangement are addressed to Mr. Even, a French merchant at Mirzapur, and a Mr. Bernier, both personal friends of his, and are dated 18th of May 1795."

I have not found any mention of Levassoult's first letter

In the meantime a deputation from the Begam's army went to Zafar-yab at Delhi and pressed him to march at their head and occupy the principality of Sardhana, which they pointed out was rightfully his, as the son of General Sombre. That young man at first hesitated, as he knew that he was no match for his sharp-witted stepmother, but on being reassured of the loyalty of the army, he could not resist the temptation of the *masnad*. At this time the news of the Begam's projected flight from Sardhana with her lover somehow leaked out at Delhi, and Zafar-yab taking courage, immediately sent a detachment of cavalry to seize the Begam and her husband.

On receiving information of Zafar-yab's advance, she fled precipitately, accompanied by Levassoult and a few faithful servants. They left the town secretly at midnight and proceeded directly towards the Ganges with a view to seeking refuge in the country of the Wazir Asaf-ud-daula, taking with them

---

to the Governor-General anywhere except the one, dated 6th May 1795. Perhaps this may be the letter which Sleeman says was his last one, and dated 30th April 1795.

their portable property—one *lakh* of Rupees in specie and jewellery worth about another *lakh*. But they had not gone far when their flight was discovered, and a pursuing column overtook them at the village of Khirwa, in the Begam's *jagir*, only five miles from her capital.*

On the approach of the pursuers Levassoult, who was accompanying the Begam's palanquin on horseback, rode up to her side and told her in a firm voice that he would rather put an end to his life than fall into the hands of the infuriated ruffians. So deeply was the Begam infatuated that she declared she would not be parted from him even in death and, to show her determination, produced a dagger from her bodice. Levassoult felt comforted, and urged the groaning palanquin bearers to hurry on; but in vain.

Levassoult was a chivalrous gentleman and was passionately devoted to his wife to whom he owed so much. He could have galloped away and thus saved

*According to Sleeman they set out for Anupshahr and the rebels intercepted them at Kabri, some 3 miles from Sardhana upon the road to Meerut.

himself, but it was not for him to leave the Begam to her fate. The insurgents came up close behind them, when suddenly a wail was heard. It was the scream of the Begam's female attendants. Levassoult hurried to the spot and, looking into the litter, found the Begam lying unconscious, her clothes stained with blood from a self-inflicted wound.

From this Levassoult inferred that she was dead, and true to his vow, he fulfilled his part of the compact to the letter. He put a pistol to his temple, pulled the trigger, and fell down lifeless from the saddle.* "The villains, who the preceding

---

* The inscription on the tomb of Col. Levassoult is not legible and the only part that can be read now is :

> *priez Dieu pour son âme; requiescat in pacem. 18th October 1795.*

Keene, who visited the Catholic cemetery at Sardhana in 1880, writes : "In the very centre of the enclosure a platform with a screen marks the resting place of poor Levassoult, with an inscription in French, recording that he died 18th October 1795, *agé de 47 ans,* and begging the passenger to *prier pour son âme*" (*Calcutta Review,* 1880).

It appears to be highly probable that the date in question is the date of erection of the tablet and not the date of Levassoult's death, which must have happened very shortly after the despatch of the Begam's letter (6th May 1795). Judging from the state of affairs, the flight of the Begam from Sardhana could not have taken place later than the end of June.

day had styled themselves his slaves, now committed every act of insult and indignity upon his corpse! For three days it lay exposed to the insults of the rabble, and was at length thrown into a ditch" (*Thomas*, p. 34).

It was now the Begam's turn to suffer at the hands of the rebels. She had stabbed herself, but her stiletto had been turned off by the ribs, without penetrating any vital part, and she had not the courage to repeat the blow. She soon recovered, only to find herself a prisoner.

The rebels turned back to Sardhana with the plunder and the captive Begam. She was taken to the old fort, and kept tied under a gun-carriage for seven days exposed to the scorching heat and a victim to the insults and jeers of the mob. She was denied food or drink, and would have perished of starvation but for the *ayas* who continued faithful to her and supplied her wants by stealth.

Zafar-yab Khan had thus obtained his heart's desire, and he celebrated his triumph with his accustomed revels and debauchery. But though he was thus outwardly rejoicing, he had evidently a secret fear that his position was not as yet consolidated, and he therefore commenced negotiating to gain the tacit approval of the British Government to the territorial power he had thus usurped.

With this object in view, he despatched two Persian letters to the British Commanding Officer at Anupshahr for transmission to the Governor-General. One of these was under the Begam's seal and dated 27th March 1796 (17 Ramzan, 1210 H.),* and the other, dated 29th March (19 Ramzan) had his own affixed to it.† The Commanding Officer, doubtful of the propriety of transmitting the letters to the Governor-General, passed them on to Wm. Palmer, the Resident with Sindhia who, in his turn, forwarded them to Sir John Shore with a covering letter, dated Fatehgarh, 23rd April 1796.

The contents of both these letters were to the same effect, making out that the rebellion was the result of Levassoult's high-handed dealings and that Zafar-yab

* *Original Letter* No. 214; *Pol. Procdgs.* 16-5-1796, No. 48.

† *Original Letter* No. 215; *Pol. Procdgs.* 16-5-1796, No. 47.

Khan had successfully rescued the Begam from an awkward situation, in recognition of which the Begam had placed Zafar-yab in sole charge of all her affairs.* The letter purporting to have been sent by the Begam was either a forgery or else she had

* " . . . . You will have heard of my situation by the newspapers. Monsr. Levassoult, to whose management I had entrusted all my concerns from a mistaken judgment, all at once, without any cause whatsoever, began to dismiss the sepoys, who had long been in my service,—experienced men, whose fidelity and attachment had been repeatedly tried—and was about to involve my affairs in ruin and disorder. But through that Providend which has ever attended me, the battalions rose in a body and Monsr. Levassoult through terror put an end to himself with a pistol. I was in consequence obliged to send for my beloved son Zafar-yab Khan and of my free will and accord I entrusted to him the whole management of my affairs as before to Monsr. Levassoult, for there is nothing in the world more precious than a son, particularly an accomplished one. My son is possessed of an acute understanding and is prospectus beyond compare. From the day of his being invested with the management of my affairs he has been solicitous even more than necessary to please me, has renewed and cemented former connections with the chiefs of the country and thereby rectified all that was amiss and happiness to afford me pleasure. My sincere attachment demands that you believe me to be among the number of your well-wishers and constantly oblige me with kind letters and also that my son may likewise be the object of your favour and regard in a greater degree even than you are pleased to consider me, and hereafter have the goodness to address to him any application you may have to make to this quarter, as this will be peculiarly gratifying to me."

been forced against her will to affix her seal to it. Sir John Shore was of the above opinion as can be easily gathered from his letter to Palmer, dated 19th May 1796, in which he remarked that, so far from countenancing Zafar-yab Khan's act of violence, he was inclined to afford her any help that he could render.*

Palmer's reply to the above letter was:

> ". . . . There can be no doubt of her being under restraint both in her person and actions, the king having repeatedly applied in quality of her adoptive father to take her under his protection, without effect. The revolution in the *jagir* was evidently a usurpation on the part of Zafar-yab Khan. It has, however, been connived at by the

* ". . . . As the purport of the letter from the Begam is so little correspondent with the circumstances under which she was deprived of the control over her jagir, I cannot but entertain a suspicion that the letter is either fictitious and framed by Zafar-yab Khan in her name or extorted from her with a view to obtain from this Government an acknowledgment of his usurped authority. Although I have no pretensions to interfere between the Begam and her son, her acknowledged attention to this Government affords her a title to any assistance which I can afford her, without the commitment of a direct interference. I not only therefore think proper to avoid giving any countenance to the violence of Zafar-yab Khan, but should be very happy to afford her any relief under the promised limitation" (*Pol. Procdgs.* 20-5-1796, No. 44.)

> Maratha Government either from indifference, or the want of opportunity to restore it to the Begam. I shall gladly embrace any safe mode of conveying your sentiments to the Begam, but I fear that she is too closely watched to admit of any correspondence reaching her but through the hands of her son."*

In the meantime the Begam was in a very precarious position indeed. She still had, however, one faithful friend left amongst her officers, who had not altogether abandoned his old mistress. This was M. Saleur, through whose intervention the Begam was released from her painful position, although still kept in confinement. Here she endeavoured to find out means for regaining her liberty, and thought of appealing to George Thomas. But he had not been favourably disposed towards her and, according to Sleeman (ii. 281), had "instigated the officers to this violence out of pique against the Begam, for her preference of the Frenchman." However, as his rival was no longer in the land of the living, the

* Letter dated 8th [4th ?] June 1796 from Wm. Palmer, Resident with Sindhia, to Sir John Shore. *Pol. Procdgs.* 20-6-1796, No. 9.

Begam thought that if she then sought his assistance he could not but respond to her call. She supposed that not only did he still love her but that he might also be grateful to his former mistress for the many favours received at her hands. "In a manner the most abject and desponding, she addressed Mr. Thomas; she stated her apprehensions of being poisoned, or otherwise put to death; affirmed that her only dependence was on him, implored him to come to her assistance, and, finally, offered to pay any sum of money the Marathas should require, on condition they would reinstate her in her jagir" (*Thomas*, p. 54).

The Begam was a good judge of character, and her calculations proved correct. The chivalrous nature of the Irish soldier was deeply moved when he learnt from her letters that Levassoult was no more and that she herself was a captive in the hands of the rebels and suffering indignities he had not dreamt of. He brushed away from his mind his ancient grudge and "by an offer of Rs. 120,000 prevailed on Bapu Sindhia [the Maratha governor of the Upper Doab] to make a movement towards

Sardhana. Convinced from his former experience, that unless he could gain over a part of the troops under Zafar-yab Khan to the Begam's interest, not only would his exertions be fruitless, but that she herself would be exposed to the greatest personal danger, he set on foot negotiations for this purpose, in which having succeeded, he marched and encamped with his whole force at the village of Khatauli, eight *kos* to the north-east of Sardhana. Here Mr. Thomas publicly gave out, that unless the Begam was reinstated in her authority, those who resisted must expect no mercy, and to give additional weight to this declaration, he apprized them, that he was acting under the orders of the Maratha chiefs" (*Thomas*, pp. 54-55). There was still, declared he, an empire, of which they were the servants and Sindhia the master; and should the Begam die, the minister would certainly disband such a disorderly brigade and resume the lands assigned for their payment.

"This intimation was at first attended with the desired effect. Part of the troops belonging to the garrison instantly mutinied, confined Zafar-yab Khan, and declared for the Begam. Mr. Thomas, however, who well knew that no reliance could be placed on the capricious temper of troops accustomed to frequent mutinies, lost no time in advancing to Sardhana, but before he reached that place, a counter revolution had already proclaimed the restoration of Samru's son.

"Escorted by only 50 horse of approved fidelity, Mr. Thomas entered the cantonments, having at the time he set out directed 400 of his infantry to follow him with all possible expedition; the arrival of the latter force was particularly fortunate, as Zafar-yab Khan on Mr. Thomas's first appearance, perceiving him slightly attended, thought he had now got him into his power, and instructed his soldiers to threaten him with instant death, but at that moment the reinforcement above-mentioned arriving, and the mutineers thinking the whole Maratha force was at hand, not only gave over their design, but now became as submissive, as they had before been insolent" (*Thomas*, pp. 55-56).

These events took place some time

in June-July 1796. Thus, the Begam regained her status after having remained under restraint for nearly a year.*

"Part of the sum stipulated to be paid to Bapu Sindhia for restoring her to authority was now paid, and the remainder promised.† An interview took

---

* "Be so good as to inform Sir John Shore that I have received authentic intelligence from my agent at Delhi that the Begam Zeb-un-nisa has recovered her authority in her *jagir* and has put her son-in-law Zafar-yab Khan in confinement. This revolution in favour of the Begam has been principally effected by an Englishman named George Thomas, who was formerly in her service and high in her confidence, but left her employ a few years since in consequence of some misunderstanding and engaged in the Maratha service. At this time he is in command of a battalion of sepoys under the orders of the *subahdar* of Delhi. It seems that he marched with his corps secretly to Sardhana where he was joined by some troops in the Begam's interest and with whom the plan for her restoration had been previously concerted and to which it is supposed that the Maratha sardars were privy and gave encouragement."—Letter, dated Fatehgarh 21st July 1796, from Wm. Palmer, Resident with Sindhia, to the Persian Translator. *Pol. Procdgs.* 5-8-1796, No. 5.

In regard to the Begam's restoration, I have followed the version of Thomas (pp. 54-56) which is quite in agreement with that given by Palmer.

† Sleeman records (ii. 283) that the officer of Sindhia, who was to have commanded the Begam's troops on her abdication, was present at the reinstallation of the Begam, and accepted "as a compensation for his disappointment, the sum of one hundred and fifty thousand Rupees, which the Begam contrived to borrow for him."

place between the Begam and the Maratha chiefs, when everything being amicably adjusted, the Maratha army quitting Sardhana repaired to their respective destinations" (*Thomas*, p. 56). The command of her own troops was entrusted to Monsr. Jean Saleur, who had not taken any part in the mutiny but, on the contrary, striven hard to bring his brother officers back to a sense of their duty.

The unfortunate usurper, Zafar-yab, robbed of all his possessions, was sent a prisoner to Delhi, where he died (*c.* 1802)* —some say, by poison. He was buried beside his father in the graveyard of Agra.

The Begam remembered with gratitude the invaluable services of Geo. Thomas as long as she lived. Later when Thomas, his fortunes wrecked, determined to set out for Europe, he went to Sardhana and left his wife—Maria,†

* Dyce Sombre places his death in 1799 (*Refutation*, p. 6). In her letter to the Governor-General, dated 4th August *1802*, the Begam says: "The only child which I had, Zafar-yab Khan, *died some time ago*" (*Original Letter* No. 323).

† According to Keegan (*Sardhana*, pp. 39, 54) the Begam on the occasion of her reinstallation, gave him a wife, one

one daughter, and three sons under the care and protection of the Begam. She gladly accepted the charge and continued to provide for them after his death, which occurred on 22nd August 1802 at Bahrampur, where he was buried in the English cemetery. She took John Thomas, the eldest son of Maria, as one of her adopted sons, and married him to the daughter of Agha Wanus, an Armenian in her service. The Begam also left in her will a sum of Rs. 44,000 for the family of George Thomas.*

The Begam realized that her marriage with Levassoult was the greatest blunder she had ever committed, and on regaining her *masnad* never again did she allow the weakness of her sex to imperil her sovereignty. The revolt of the soldiers was not wholly unwarranted and "the troops in this mutiny pretended nothing more than a desire to vindicate the honour of their old commander, Sombre,

---

of her chief maids of honour. This young lady's name was Maria, and her parentage was French.

* Maria, wife of Geo. Thomas Rs. 7,000; John Thomas and his wife Joanna [Sohagun Begam] Rs. 18,000 and 7,000; Jacob Thomas and Geo. Thomas Rs. 10,000 and 2,000.

which had, they said, been compromised by the illicit intercourse between Levassoult and his widow . . . Some grave old native gentlemen who were long in her service have told me [Sleeman] that they believed there really was too much of truth in the story which excited the troops to mutiny on that occasion—her too great intimacy with the gallant young Frenchman. God forgive them for saying so of a lady whose salt they had eaten for so many years" (Sleeman, ii. 283).

The Begam was really penitent and expiated for her thoughtless conduct with earnestness and sincerity. After her restoration she did all she could to keep the memory of her first husband ever green in her mind. She retained to the last the name of Sombre, her first husband, and remained silent ever afterwards on the subject of her secret marriage with Levassoult, which was known only to a very few men of the time. She stipulated in her deed of gift that her adopted son and heir—Mr. David Ochterlony Dyce—should identify himself as one of the family of Sombre by adding that name to his own.

APPENDIX *A*

COLONEL LEVASSOULT'S LETTER TO LIEUTENANT-COLONEL J. M'GOWAN, COMMANDING AT ANUPSHAHR.

Sirdhanah, April 2nd, 1795.

Sir,

The letter you have been pleased to honour me with has reached this day, and in conformity to the desire and direction of the Begam, I beg leave to trouble you once more on the same subject.

The sole views and motive of the Begam are confined at her strong desire for retirement. Should it have been the same in this country as in Europe, her resignation would have been effected without any bad consequences in asking simply for it ; but you cannot but know perfectly well that a chief in Hindustan keeps difficulty to himself when he is without soldiers or attendants ; hence the danger to let his intention be made public, should it be to retire and serve no more.

Maratha amity cannot be hurt by the removal of the Begam into British possessions, should they have not the unjust and illegal scheme of spoiling her of her property. The arms, the guns, the whole of the furniture and armament for 5,000 men, are the property not of the Government, but of the Begam. Her wages as a partizan, are fixed lastly by Sindhia at Rs. 50,000 by the month, or six lakhs for a year ; the payment of that allowance is fixed on eight provinces or parganas, which have been delivered for the purpose of receiving it.

Now the Begam, by her removal, pure and simple, subtracts nothing at the authority or at the property of the Maratha Government. Her party is paid regularly each month the recolt [harvest] is ready ; her battalions are upon duty, and the whole are in the best order.

Her property on the vow of a man of honour amounts only at one lakh in ready cash. She has but very little jewels ; her meuble cannot be either carried away with her or sold ; therefore you may judge yourself whether, after a command of eighteen years, the Begam can be called rich ; with a capital or property so mediocre, of having frustrated either the Government or any people whatsoever.

She is absolutely fatigued by the duties and cares of the military possession which has been the object of her attendance for a space of eighteen years. She resorts at your friendship, because she cannot by any way whatsoever make her intention known either to the Government to which she is subordinate, or to her own soldiers, without exposing herself to many dangers.

She cannot employ a Persian writer for the same reason, but if you may be desirous to have the matter plainly and more properly explained, she will do herself the pleasure to send to you a gentleman who shall give you all satisfactory answers you may ask. I cannot myself have this honour, for the place committed to my charges permit not my being absent ; and although my writing bad English, I am not able to speak or understand a word of it in conversation, by my being perfectly unacquainted with pronunciation. Were you so good to command him, the above-mentioned gentleman shall be ordered at you from Tappal, where he is upon a command, and as your friendship towards the Begam, contrive some means of serving her desire for retirement. She flatters herself that you will be so kind to communicate the same, and to indicate the measure which shall be taken and the proper persons to which the Begam shall address herself by your friendly assistance and medium. I have the honour to be with respect,

Sir,

Your most humble and obedient servant,

A. Levassoult

(*Refutation*, pp. 443-45).

CHAPTER VI

SARDHANA UNDER BRITISH PROTECTION

At the time when General Sombre founded the principality of Sardhana, the British, although well established in Bengal, were not in a position to contend with the Indian Powers ruling in Upper India and the Deccan. Warren Hastings had the greatest difficulty in breaking up the confederacy of the Southern States organized by the Nizam with the object of destroying the growth of the English Power (1779). The only Maratha chief friendly to the British was Mahadji Sindhia, whose army was then being organized by officers delegated by Hastings. It was through Mahadji's mediation that the treaty of Salbai with the Puna Court was signed (1782), for which Hastings was really grateful to him. This transaction greatly enhanced Sindhia's influence, and his power grew rapidly. His armies—commanded and instructed by European generals—placed him in the position of a king-maker in

Hindustan. The British did not interfere with the growth of his power, because as a matter of fact they could not then afford to quarrel with such a formidable chieftain. (Smith's *Oxford Hist. of India*, pp. 585-36). This friendly relation with Mahadji and his successor Daulat Rao Sindhia was continued throughout the administration of Lord Cornwallis and Sir John Shore.

From the beginning of her career Begam Samru began to treat the English as a friendly Power, and did not hesitate to help them in their need. We learn from Persian letters,* addressed by the Begam to the Hon'ble Charles Stuart, a member of the Supreme Council, that Col. Stuart, a military officer attached to the frontier station of Anupshahr, had been taken prisoner† by the Sikh chief Bhanga

* Two letters from her received at Fort William on 15th November, 1791—*Abstract of Pers. Letters Received*, 1791, Nos. 309 & 310. Palmer to Govr.-Genl. dated 13 Feb. 1792; Begam to Palmer, recd. at Fort William, 23 Feb.—*Political Consultations* 18-4-1792, Nos. 13, 15.

† "April 1790:—From the English camp in Anupshahr an English officer named 'Istur' had gone two or four *kos* to hunt. The Sikhs, who kept news of it, sent 1,000 troops (under Karam Singh) and captured him. The Englishman offered Rs. 20,000 as ransom but the Sikhs demanded one

Singh and that the Begam had, in response to Major Palmer's request, secured his release on 24th October 1791 (25 Safar, 1206 H.) by paying a ransom of Rs. 15,000 for him. She advanced 10 miles to meet him on the way and escort him to her place. This demonstration of friendship on the Begam's part was welcomed by the British Government* and paved the way for a closer relationship between them. The Governor-General in Council recorded a resolution on 18th April 1792, that

---

lakh" (p. 145). "He has now been released and sent to Delhi after a bond (*nisa*) with a promise to pay sixty thousand Rupees had been executed through the mediation of Begam Samru. Four Englishmen and one Company of soldiers have come from Anupshahr to escort him back to English territory" (p. 25). *Dilli-yethil Marathanchin Rajkaranen*, ii. 25 & 145.

* "......... It is with sensible pleasure that I learn this happy circumstance is owing to your friendship and exertions. I have to offer my sincere acknowledgments for this instance of your attachment, which will ever be remembered by me and all the members of this Government as an additional instance of the good disposition you have on all occasions manifested towards this Government. I shall not fail to inform Earl Cornwallis of the circumstance, who will no doubt be equally gratified by it as myself. I have since had the pleasure to learn that the Colonel has safely arrived at Anupshahr."—Letter, dated 20th December 1791, addressed by Hon. C. Stuart to the Begam. See *Vol. of Eng. Trans. of Pers. Letters Written*, 22-12-1791, No. 234; also *Pol. Con.* 29-10-1832, No. 72.

"Major Palmer be instructed to remit the sum disbursed on this occasion by Zeb-un-nisa (being Rs. 15,000) to that lady, and that Mr. Stuart be requested to send her, on the part of Government, such a present as he may think most proper, accompanied by a letter containing suitable acknowledgments of her laudable exertions in behalf of Lt.-Col. Stuart" (*Pol. Con.* 18-4-1792, No. 16).

Sir John Shore, in his letter dated 22nd May 1794, requested her help in capturing the deserters from the British forces at Cawnpur and Fatehgarh.* At the time of her flight from Sardhana the Begam contemplated retiring into the territory of the friendly British, and her correspondence with Sir John Shore and other officials brought her into closer touch with them. She remembered with gratitude the courtesy of the British and continued to exchange friendly letters with them.

After the retirement of Hastings the British Government followed a policy of

---

* *Vol. of Eng. Trans. of Pers. Letters Written*, 22-5-1794, No. 166. In *Refutation* (pp. 358-59) this letter is wrongly given as "Dated 1797."

non-intervention with the Native Powers and refrained from conquests and alliances except in defence of their existing possessions. They were, however, consolidating their hold on their possessions, and when Lord Wellesley took over charge in May 1798, he found the British Power firmly established.

The policy of the new Governor-General was mainly directed towards two objects. The first was the elevation of the British Government to the position of the paramount Power in India, or in his own words "to unite the principal Native States in the bond of peace under the protection of the British Power." And the next was, the fullest utilization of Indian strength to resist Napoleon's bid for world power which threatened the existence of the British dominion in India. With these avowed objects he started "to make annexations right and left without any qualms of conscience." (*O. H. I.*, p. 580).

Begam Samru, who had been an interested spectator of the rise of the English Power, naturally felt alarmed at the rapid advance of the British and the fall of one Indian principality after another during the vigorous campaigns of Lord Lake in Northern India and of General Arthur Wellesley in the Deccan. The internal affairs of the Marathas at this period presented a scene of terrible confusion. Grant Duff, writing of the year 1799, describes a state of absolute anarchy in the Peshwa's territory where the Peshwa, Sindhia, the *Bais* or ladies of his family, the Rajah of Kolhapur, and other parties were all fighting one with the other.* The Begam clearly foresaw that a conflict between her overlord, Sindhia and the British was inevitable, and she had no delusion as to its result. Her friendliness towards the English had excited the suspicion of Genl. Perron, the chief of Sindhia's forces, who began secretly to disaffect the Begam's troops with a view to bringing about her downfall. She saw that if she remained an ally of the Marathas she would be equally ruined whichever side might win. Having nothing to lose and everything to gain from the victory of the British, which

* The twelfth volume of Marathi historical letters published by Kharé in 1924 shows that Puna was a hell under Baji Rao II.

seemed the more probable, she decided to throw in her lot with them and started making secret overtures to them as early as January 1802* in order to safeguard her interests. In her letter of 4th August 1802 (4 Rabi-us-sani, 1217 H.)† she offered to place her territory and troops at the disposal of the Governor-General in exchange for his protection. In a second letter, dated 1st February 1803, the Begam says:

> "As I am from the bottom of my heart attached to the British Government, I feel an irresistible desire that your Lordship should preserve me, though absent, in your remembrance. Adverting to these my declared sentiments, whatever plans your Lordship may have in contemplation, your Lordship will in the first instance communicate them to me, that I may have an opportunity of manifesting the sincerity of my heart by affording the aid of my co-operation in your measures. *I have a force stationed in the*

* Letter, received on 10th Jany. 1802, from Zeb-un-nisa Begam to Lord Wellesley. This is a complimentary letter notifying her mission of Hakim Muhammad Jafar to attend the Governor-General on her part.—*Vol. of Eng. Trans. of Pers. Letters Received*, 10-1-1802, No. 5.

† This letter was received at Fort William on 9 Sep. 1802. See Appendix *B*.

Deccan which your Lordship must consider as awaiting your orders."*

This offer of submission and help was acknowledged with pleasure,† but owing to diplomatic reasons the British were unable to avail themselves of her forces immediately.‡

After the political degradation of the Nizam, Tipu, and other rulers of Southern India between 1798 and 1800 a complete alteration took place in the relations between the British and the Maratha States. The policy of non-interference in

* *Vol. of Eng. Trans. of Pers. Letters Received,* 27-3-1803, No. 71. The date of this letter, *viz.,* 1st February 1803, is given in Persian character on the envelope, see *Original Letter* No. 143.

† Letter, dated 20th May 1803, from Lord Wellesley to Zeb-un-nisa Begam.—*Vol. of Eng. Trans. of Pers. Letters Written,* 20-5-1803, No. 77.

‡ "But with regard to the situation in which Begam Samru stood, relative to Sindhia, her proposition, however desirable it might be, was unacceptable by reason of the peace and amity at that time subsisting between the British and Sindhia. That he might not violate public faith, the Governor-General had always refused her proposition; however, apprizing the Begam, that if an opportunity presented itself, the Governor-General should be happy to have it in his power to accept the proofs of her attachment to the British Government."—Wellesley's *Despatches to the Secret Committee of the Hon. Court of Directors,* dated 12th April 1804, para 341.

Maratha affairs had ceased to be practicable, because the Maratha chiefs always had claims outstanding against both Haidarabad and Mysore for the realization of *chauth* and on other accounts, and their troops were being maintained by the plunder obtained at the expense of their neighbours. Therefore, the only possible alternatives left open to the Governor-General were either the abandonment of all conquests, or the adoption of such measures as would force the Maratha Governments to acquiesce in a state of general peace and tranquillity. Lord Wellesley set about to consider the means by which he might attain the latter object. The prospect of success in such an endeavour was not bright, as Maratha institutions and ideas were fundamentally incompatible with Wellesley's policy of a confederacy of Native States under British protection. (*O. H. I.*, p. 595). In the course of his intervention in the affairs of the Peshwa, which ended in the restoration of Baji Rao II under British protection, according to the treaty of Bassein, the attitude of the Peshwa and the Bhonslé Rajah of Nagpur gave Lord

Wellesley cause to expect hostilities from them in the near future. He decided to make use of the Begam's proffered help, and wrote to her on 22nd July 1803 in the following words:

> "The present state of affairs enables me to avail myself of your friendly offers of assistance and I am persuaded that your influence will be exerted with promptitude and effect to promote the interests of the British Government. The detailed conditions on which I am disposed to offer you the friendship of the Honourable Company will be communicated to you by His Excellency the Commander-in-chief [Lord Lake] who is in full possession of my sentiments on this subject."*

At the same time Lord Wellesley instructed Lord Lake as to the lines on which negotiations were to be carried on with her.†

Although by this time war with Sindhia had been finally decided upon, it was not declared until the 6th of August 1803. The exchange of letters between the Begam and the British Government

* *Vol. of Eng. Trans. of Pers. Letters Written*, 22-7-1803, No. 97.

† Letter, dated 28th July 1803, from Marquis Wellesley to Lord Lake.—*Wellesley Despatches*, iii. 242-44.

went on, but no actual service was asked of her until the 7th of September 1803. In his letter of that date (*Refutation*, p. 362) Lord Lake required her to furnish *bona fides* of her overtures by providing him with some boats of the *dongah* (canoe) kind and by placing her troops, which were then serving with the armies of Sindhia, at the disposal of Genl. Arthur Wellesley, or at least to observe neutrality by recalling them.

Shortly after this, the battle of Assaye was fought (23 Sept. 1803) where Sindhia's army met with a severe defeat. Five,* out of the six battalions of the Begam, and 15 guns under the command of Col. Saleur, had taken part in this battle on the side of Sindhia. As regards the demeanour of these battalions in action the following extract is sufficiently illustrative:

> "It is a remarkable thing, and much to the credit of the Begam's troops, that some four or five of her battalions were the only part of Sindhia's army that went off unbroken from the field of Assaye: they were charged

* For the "Roll of the Detachment under the command of Col. Saleur," see *Secret Consultation* 21-11-1805, No. 52A.

by our [British] cavalry towards the close of the day, but without effect ; Col. Maxwell, who commanded, being killed in the charge by a grape-shot" (Skinner, i. 286*n*).

The Begam issued instructions to Col. Saleur, in accordance with Lord Lake's request, early in October,* but that officer experienced great difficulty and risk in giving effect to her orders. The battalions, however, "left Sindhia's camp at Burhanpur on 14th October 1803 (27 Jamadi-us-sani, 1218 H.)".† "At the time they left the Maratha camp they consisted of five battalions and a party of horse"‡ under the command of Col. Saleur who,

* "Prior to this *about a month and a half ago* I issued orders to you, requiring you to disengage yourself from the service of the Southern chief and join the British forces. Eight days, afterwards, I repeated those orders; again, on the 27th of the present month of Rajab [13 November], I renewed them in terms the most peremptory. These reiterated orders were forwarded to you in succession by two *harkarahs*. Instructions were also transmitted to you, through the British Commander-in-chief."—Translation of a Persian letter addressed by the Begam to Col. Saleur dated the last day of Rajab 1218 H.=16 Nov. 1803. *Sect. Procdgs.* 2-3-1804, No. 183A. See also Nos. 183 and 183B.

† Statement accompanying letter dated 20 Sept. 1805, from Mr. G. D. Guthrie to N. B. Edmonstone. *Sect. Procdgs.* 21-11-1805, No. 52A.

‡ Letter from Mr. G. D. Guthrie dated Sept. 1805, to Col. J. Malcolm. *Sect. Procdgs.* 21-11-1805, No. 53.

on his arrival at Deeg [on 15th Decr.] received orders agreeably to which he joined Col. Ball's detachment at Kanund. They served the British general up to 31st May, Col. Pœthod having relieved Col. Saleur in their command, on account of his ill-health on 13th February.* They afterwards "marched to Tappal to join the Commander-in-chief, but returned to Sardhana without having" done so.†

In the meantime the Begam sent Hakim Muhammad Jafar‡ as her agent to Lord Lake. Evidently as a result of the conversations between them a secret treaty was concluded under which the Begam transferred her allegiance to the British, who were at this time in

---

* *Secret Procdgs.* 21-11-1805, No. 52A.

The Begam's claim for payment on account of the service of her troops dating from their departure from Burhanpur was admitted by the British Government in November 1805, see *Secret Procdgs.* 21-11-1805, Nos. 52A, 53 and 55; *Vol. of Eng. Trans. of Pers. Letters Received,* 26-2-1804, No. 48.

† Letter from Mr. G. D. Guthrie dated Septr. 1805, to Col. J. Malcolm. *Secret Procdgs.* 21-11-1805, No. 53.

‡ Lake to the Begam, undated.

From the context it appears that this letter was addressed to the Begam after the battle of Assaye was fought on 23 Sept. 1803. (*Refutation,* pp. 411-12).

possession of Delhi and the surrounding tracts, and she was allowed to retain her territory and status as a jagirdar of the British Government.* Lord Lake also asked the Begam to write to her friend Ranjit Singh, the ruler of Lahor, to keep his troops out of the districts of Saharanpur, Budeah, and others which he was then engaged in settling.

It appears that at this time certain conquered parganas in the district of Saharanpur were temporarily committed to the management of the Begam; and that she was in charge of them during the continuance of the Maratha war.†

Prior to these events Lord Wellesley had definitely formulated his policy as regards the relations to be established between the Begam and the British

---

* Lake to the Begam, dated 29-10-1803. (*Ibid.* 412).

† Letter, dated Sept. 1805, from Guthrie to Malcolm, 10th para. *Sect. Procdgs.* 21-11-1805, No. 53.

For the statement, showing the land and Sayer revenue and sundry other items collected by the Begam exhibiting the difference between the accounts transmitted by her and those given by the qanungoes of *zila* Saharanpur, see *Sect. Procdgs.* 21-11-1805, No. 52B. The collections made by the Begam were chiefly on account of the balance of 1210 H. [1795-96] and 1211 H. [1796-97].

Government. Originally his idea was to "commute her *jagir* for a suitable stipend, the extent of which must be regulated by the profits which she actually derives from her territorial possessions, and by the importance of the services which the British Government may derive from the exertion of her aid and influence."*

It was extremely important then that the whole Doab, including the territory occupied by the Begam, should come under direct British rule, but how this could be best effected was left to Lord Lake to decide. After a thorough study of the Begam's disposition and the power she wielded in the province, Lake recommended that it would be better to propose an exchange of territories, which arrangement was sanctioned by Lord Wellesley.†

Sindhia's forces having been overcome both in Northern and Southern India and the British being in firm

---

* Lord Wellesley to Lord Lake, dated 28th July 1803. *Wellesley Despatches*, iii. 242-44.

† Letter, dated 11th October 1803, from the Secretary to Govt. in the Sect Dept. to the Agent of the Governor-General.

possession of all his territories east of the Jamuna, Lord Lake wrote to the Begam on the 29th October, 1803:

> "Immediately on receiving this letter, and in accordance with the tenor of the deeds granted to you by the present (Government) you will come alone to my presence, as some matters are to be verbally mentioned to you; and keep your troops ready prepared forward, that there may be no confusion when an order is received" (*Refutation*, p. 412).

At this meeting Lake no doubt proposed that she should give up her present possessions in the Doab and accept lands to the west of the Jamuna to hold as an independent sovereign. She readily agreed to this proposal, hoping thereby to attain a more exalted rank and other benefits as an ally of the premier Power in India. She was directed to see Lt.-Col. Ochterlony, the Resident at Delhi, and arrange the terms of the proposed exchange. She visited Delhi on the 12th of November, and in a letter written to Lord Wellesley, within a week of the visit, she says:

> "It has been intimated to me by Col. Ochterlony that Commissioners have been appointed to

settle the affairs of the Doab. It therefore occurs to my mind that as difficulties might arise between me and the Commissioners in the exercise of their authority in the vicinity of the *mahals,* which constitute my *jagir,* it would be prudent to provide against the occurrence of them since it is my primary study to promote your Excellency's satisfaction and I should be utterly unable to support the weight of the displeasure of the Commissioners. Under these circumstances I hereby, of my own free will and accord, relinquish my *jagir,* which I have possessed for the space of 30 years, and for which my partiality and affection is equal to that which I bear for my native land, and on which I have moreover expended large sums of money in erecting buildings for my own residence and the accommodation of my troops ; notwithstanding these powerful reasons, however, every one of which forbid the act, I readily resign it into the hands of the Company......Let territory be assigned to me in *jagir* on the other side of the Jamuna in lieu of the *mahals,* the possession of which I have relinquished. At the same time I hope that the territory which may be so assigned to me, may be compact and undivided, with a view to its successful management" (*Sect. Procdgs.* 2-3-1804, No. 183C).

Although due to recent conquests considerable territories to the west of the

Jamuna* were available out of which a suitable principality could be formed for her, the prevailing unrest greatly hampered the speeding up of the transfer. On the other hand, Lord Wellesley's policy demanded an immediate settlement of the Begam's territories, and therefore on 23rd December 1803 he wrote in reply a letter to the Begam reaffirming the offer previously made and urging the immediate surrender of her estates under guarantee of compensation for any loss she might incur therefrom:

> "The sentiments expressed in your letter [received on 5-12-1803] and the judicious and amicable course of proceeding which you have adopted on the present occasion, have confirmed the sense which I have long entertained of your attachment to the interests of the British Government.........I am particularly gratified by your ready

* "The territory placed at the disposal of the British Govt. by the glorious success of our arms at the battle of Delhi, furnished us with the means of assigning to the Begam a territory on the western part of the Jamuna instead of the jagir which she possessed in the Doab." Para 55, Wellesley's *Despatches to the Secret Committee of the Hon'ble Court of Directors*, 12th April 1804. (*Refutation*, p. 424).

acquiescence in the suggestion conveyed to you under my orders by His Excellency the Commander-in-chief, for the recall of your battalions serving with the army of Daulat Rao Sindhia and in the assignment of territory on the western side of the Jamuna in exchange for your present possessions in the Doab. With a view to manifest the sense which I entertain of your meritorious conduct on this occasion and to afford you ample compensation for the relinquishment of your present *jagir,* I have resolved to guarantee to you the independent possession of the territory which will be assigned to you under the proposed arrangement without any other condition than that of affording to the British Government the aid of your troops whenever it may be required, and of submitting to the arbitration of the British Government any differences which may eventually arise between you and any other State or chieftain. H. E. the Commander-in-chief will adopt as soon as possible the necessary measures for transferring to you a portion of territory on the western side of the Jamuna equivalent to that which you have ceded in the Doab. I trust, however, that you will not delay the actual cession of your present jagir, to the authority of the British Government, until the assignment of an equivalent portion of territory, which must necessarily occupy some time before it can be effected. You will receive ample compensation from the British Govt. for any loss of revenue which may be occasioned by the delay in selecting and transferring to your authority the districts to be assigned to you on the western side of the Jamuna."*

This letter had a very disturbing effect on the Begam's mind. She had seen promises made and broken every day of her life, and therefore it was not easy for her to believe that Lord Wellesley really meant to keep his word and was not trying to rob her of her lands by a trick.

She had been under the impression that as soon as she would give up her former possessions, the English would grant her new territories; and she was therefore surprised that this was not to be the case. The bitter disappointment felt by the Begam on being thus summarily called upon to deliver up her possessions may be realized from the following letter, addressed to Lt.-Col. Ochterlony, on 3rd February 1804:

"You have written to me to evacuate and deliver over the districts of Sardhana etc. which has been my residence for a length of years

---

* *Vol. of Eng. Trans. of Pers. Letters Written*, 23-12-1803, No. 136; *Refutation*, p. 416 (wrongly dated 22nd Decr. 1803).

and on which I have expended lakhs of Rupees in buildings and habitations, to the *amils* of the English gentlemen immediately on their arrival. My brother, it is proper you should consider that when I go away from here, I require a place to stay in, where I may reside with my family and dependents. There are near a thousand destitute persons and lame and blind people in this district for whom a place of abode is necessary. From the commencement until the present time no gentleman invested with authority in this country has disgraced me in this manner. At the period that the English gentlemen have acquired possession of Hindustan I rejoiced that from a consideration of my being of the same race with theirs I should by some means or other be exalted in rank but the contrary has happened for they have required of me several districts possessed by me for 30 years. What may not happen to the rest?... If it be the intention of the gentlemen by some means or other to dispossess me, what occasion is there for preserving appearances? Do you my brother come and having laid hold of my hand turn me out of my abode. The world is not narrow and I am not lame. I will sit down in some retired corner and pass my time in solitude" (*Sect. Procdgs.* 2-3-1804, No. 252).

On receipt of the above letter, Lt.-Col.

Ochterlony hastened to explain matters to her and by dint of perseverance and frequent explanations persuaded her to believe that the British Government meant her no harm. Her enemies were busy at that time trying to make mischief between her and the British. Of these attempts the most remarkable one was that by means of a forged letter which purported to have been written by her to Holkar.* She consented at last, although

* "I was gratified by the receipt of your letter the object of which became manifest to me from the writings of Shaikh Qudratullah. It is fit that you consider me your sister, absorbed in a desire to gratify your inclinations, for the bonds of friendship have long acquired strength between us. I rejoice at your intention of marching to this quarter, but as they have military and artillery stores along with them in abundance, it is not proper for you to come to action with them, but you should encamp ten or eleven *kos* from them, harass them with a predatory war, destroy the country, and prevent supplies etc. reaching them, that it may be difficult for them to provide for their safety. I am every way ready, and your ally from my heart and soul. Consider all the Sikhs and Jats, who are united with me, ready to join you. Make me constantly happy by acquainting me with the state of your friendship, your designs, and the place where your army is encamped, that I may follow the same path. You will receive many letters from me (enclosed) in amulets."—Translation of a Persian letter undated, from Zeb-un-nisa Begam to Jaswant Rao Holkar. *Sect. Procdgs.* 12 April, 1804, No. 61.

Major Thorn's opinion on this letter also supports our

grudgingly, to surrender her provinces with the exception of the pargana of Sardhana.

In her letter accepting the British terms she vigorously denied the charge of treachery and secret plotting with Holkar:

> "I am willing to do according to your advice and deliver up my provinces. I only ask that until other countries will be allowed to me in exchange, that the pargana of Sardhana will remain to me ; the revenue of which I agree to be deducted from the sum which will be given to me to pay for my troops and when other place shall be granted to me for my residence and safety, I will deliver it up at the same time. I would do it now, but I am sure that your *amil* commanding the town and I remaining in the *chauni* always some complaints he would make against, right, or wrong.

---

contention that this letter was a forgery: "This document was calculated to create hostility against the Begam, and thereby probably of driving that extraordinary woman into an alliance with Holkar, out of revenge and self-defence" (p. 332).

Even Lord Lake, when forwarding this document to the Governor-General, under cover of his letter, dated Camp Hindoun 28th Feby. 1804, remarked: "This letter, though her seal is affixed to it, may possibly be a forgery."—*Sect. Procdgs.* 12-4-1804, No. 59.

I am very sorry to hear that it is reported that I do keep on correspondence with Jaswant Rao Holkar. I assure you, and you may inform yourself that since the formation of my party, which is for these 40 years past, no person yet can charge me of *treachery*, therefore, as I consider you to be a particular friend of mine, I hope you will make enquiries, and to inform yourself from whom this false report is given, and to persuade any person of the contrary, that does believe it. I enclose you three letters that I have received, from Kabul, they are in my name. However, I don't know their contents and I fear that some enemies of mine would charge me also of keeping correspondence with the king of Kabul ; this is the reason that I send them to you for to be read."*

The Begam appears to have taken offence at being charged with secret negotiations with the enemy. She had for a long time enjoyed great influence amongst the neighbouring chieftains and naturally their envoys attended her Court. But this did not necessarily mean that she was engaged in intriguing with them. When, in the beginning, she had come forward

---

* Begam to Col. Ochterlony, dated 23-2-1804.—*Sect. Procdgs.* 12-4-1804, No. 64.

of her own accord, to throw her lot in with the British, she was prepared to deal straight with them, expecting the same treatment at their hands. Had Lord Wellesley acceded to the request of the Begam for an immediate assignment of territories, instead of indulging in blundering diplomacy, he would have found in her an influential and strong ally and saved himself much trouble and anxiety, to say nothing of the cost of military operations in the province. As a matter of fact, the obvious advantage of conciliating the Begam had long been apparent to the officers who were directly in touch with her and they had all along advised Lord Wellesley to adopt this course, but without success. Even as late as 10th December 1804 Archibald Seton, the Agent to the Governor-General, reported:

> "As the situation of the Begam both from the geographical position of her country, and from the nature of her military strength, is or appears to me to be, such as to render her either a most useful ally or a very troublesome enemy, without the possibility of her ever becoming formidable as a neighbouring Power, I should imagine that the conciliating her might in the present

state of affairs be a simple and effectual means of restoring and preserving the tranquillity of the upper part of the Doab. Her force is said to consist of nine battalions of infantry and 40 guns. These, if subsidized by Government, and opposed to the Sikhs, might as far as I can judge, completely prevent their committing depredations in the British territories and, by insuring the realization of the collections, greatly enhance the value of the highly capable district now in question" (*Sect. Procdgs.* 7-3-1805, No. 424).

The indefinite delay in handing over to her the territories promised in exchange and frequent accusations against her loyalty gradually undermined her faith in the British. About the middle of 1804, Holkar, in conjunction with the Rajah of Bharatpur and the Sikh chiefs of the Lower Panjab, started a vigorous campaign which imperilled the British forces in the Doab. As they considered her assistance of great value to them, they played upon the fears of the Begam, hoping to receive active help from her. The Begam though discontented did not dare to declare openly against the British, as she was still doubtful about the ability of Holkar and his confederates to stand against the British Power. She therefore abstained from actively helping either party, and, although remaining openly an ally of the British, carried on secret negotiations with the enemy in order to remain in the good graces of whichever party might ultimately come into power. The efforts of the Sikhs and their allies were attended with a certain amount of success. In October 1804 Saharanpur fell into the hands of the Sikhs, and Col. Burn was forced to retreat. The Collector, Mr. G. D. Guthrie, was taken prisoner by Sher Singh. The Begam took this opportunity to prove her attachment to the British by securing the liberation of the Collector.*

Holkar and Ranjit Singh tried their utmost to induce her to declare in their favour, and even went to the length of exaggerating their strength and the advantages gained by Jaswant Rao Holkar over the British army, and alleging that he was going to receive reinforcements from Jodhpur, Jaipur and Kota.†

---

* "The Sikhs in the Upper Doab"—G. R. C. Williams, B. C. S., *Calcutta Review*, vol. lxi. (1875), p. 54.

† Letter, dated 26-12-1804, from Seton to the Secy. to Govt. *Secret Procdgs.* 7-3-1805, No. 435.

Rumours of this intrigue reached the ears of the British authorities and caused much alarm.* In his letter of 28th December, 1804 Archibald Seton writes:

> "From my knowledge of what had taken place at Sardhana and from what I had heard of the arts which had been practised to work upon the fears of the Begam and to impress her with a belief that the British Government had it in contemplation to reduce her power, annihilate her consequence, and degrade her from the rank which she has hitherto maintained, I was rather *concerned* than *surprised,* at receiving intelligence last night that she had accepted the terms which were offered to her by Ranjit Singh, *viz.,* the monthly payment of a lakh of Rupees, and the delivery to her of one of his forts. The intelligence has this day been confirmed to me by Mr. Guthrie, with the additional circumstance that distrustful of the fidelity of her European officers, the Begam had given the command of her troops to native sardars. I think it very probable that she will immediately march to Saharanpur in order to attack, or at least to harass and annoy Col. Burn" (*Sect. Procdgs.* 7-3-1805, No. 437).

* Lake to Zeb-un-nisa Begam, dated 16 Dec. 1804; Letter (received 29-12-1804) from the Begam to Lake.—*Sect. Procdgs.* 7-3-1805, Nos. 294 & 295.

She did not, however, actually march out of Sardhana, as she was evidently dallying with both parties till she saw the result of the siege of Deeg. The capture of the fortress of Deeg by the British on the Christmas morning of 1804, prevented her from making an open declaration against them* but she continued her threatening attitude which seriously hindered Lord Lake's operations.

When the troubles were at their highest, Col. Ochterlony addressed a letter to her requesting her to forward some stores from Sardhana to Saharanpur under escort of her own troops, and in reply she promised compliance with his request. Ochterlony's reasons for the writing of this letter† were as follows:

> "I was the more induced to this step as in the event of their compliance it would appear to the public that she had at last made her

* "My *harkarah* reports this day that the Begam Samru has positively forbidden her troops speaking on the subject of a march and I have not a doubt that the order originates in our success at Deeg."—Letter, dated 29-12-1804, from Ochterlony to the Governor-General. *Sect. Procdgs.* 31-1-1805, No. 245.

† Letter, dated 15-12-1804, from Col. Ochterlony, the Resident at Delhi, to the Governor-General. *Sect. Procdgs.* 31-1-1805, No. 236.

election in our favour and this seeming declaration I judged of importance, as her influence in this quarter is greater than can be well imagined and her indecision is certainly one great cause of the disturbances in the upper districts, if not the primary cause of the irruption of the Sikhs."*

He strongly believed that the restoration of her former *jagir* during her life was all that was needed to win the Begam over and he urged the Governor-General to do so:

"By our success she is afraid of the loss of her *parganas* and of the disbandment of her troops and such is her desire of power that I am perfectly convinced she would encounter any odds to retain both in their present state ; on the contrary, I believe that assurances of their integrity during her life would immediately induce her to declare in our favour, but at present she considers all assistance to us, as accelerating her own downfall" (*Sect. Procdgs.* 31-1-1805, No. 236).

* "The Begam having written repeated letters desiring me to send confidential persons on my part to her, I have despatched Lala Dhokul Singh to the Begam for the purpose of settling affairs.........If the negotiations with the Begam should be conducted to a favourable issue, I shall direct my march towards your district. On this point, however, keep your mind at ease."—Trans. of a letter from Ranjit Singh of Lahor to Sambanath Tahsildar of Saharanpur. *Vol.*

In spite of these urgent representations, the Governor-General insisted upon the speedy transfer of the Begam's *jagir* and her early removal with her troops beyond the Doab. Only in case of extreme emergency, should such arise, was the Commander-in-chief given the power to confirm the Begam in her present *jagir*, and even then it would be necessary to stipulate for the reduction of her forces and the replacement of her French officers by British.* The emergency referred to was probably an expected outbreak of fresh hostilities with the Marathas, encouraged by the failure of Lord Lake's operations against Bharatpur. As the Rajah of Bharatpur capitulated in the beginning of April 1805, the emergency contemplated did not arise and the Begam's affairs were left in the same unsettled state as before. The root of the trouble can be traced to Lord Wellesley's obtuseness in not taking the

---

of Eng. Trans. of Pers. Letters Received, 18-3-1805, No. 69, p. 227.

* Letter, dated 15th Feby. 1805, from N. B. Edmonstone, Secy to Government, to Lt.-Col. Ochterlony, Resident at Delhi. *Sect. Procdgs.* 28-3-1805, No. 157. See Appendix *C*.

Begam's natural thoughts into consideration; moreover, his policy of declaring war on the Native States on the slightest pretext in order to expand the British empire, naturally led the Begam to put little faith in mere promises of future favours. If Lord Wellesley had not been recalled within a few months it is probable that the Begam would have been forced to deliver up her former territories.

In July 1805 Lord Cornwallis came out for the second time as Governor-General, pledged to a policy of conciliation. His attention was drawn to the Doab, and Lord Lake, who was fully acquainted with the situation, gave it as his opinion that under the new policy of preserving peace in the country, "it is particularly necessary to conciliate the Begam Samru, and to inspire her with a just confidence in the favour and protection of the British Government. Adverting to the reasons which are supposed to have chiefly caused the Begam to behave in the equivocal manner she has lately done, His Excellency is of opinion that the most likely means of retaining her in her attachment to the

British State, will be to give her a most positive assurance that she shall during life remain in the possession of the *jagir* in the Doab *on the same terms she now holds it.*"*

Accordingly Lord Cornwallis wrote that memorable letter of 16th August 1805 which reinstated the Begam in her principality of Sardhana:

"I have had the satisfaction to learn that the general tenor of your conduct since you were placed under the protection of the British Power, has been consistent with the duties of fidelity, and I have been peculiarly gratified by the information of your prompt and successful exertions in rescuing Mr. Guthrie, the Collector of Saharanpur, from a situation of imminent danger by the aid of your troops, and of your kind and liberal treatment of that gentleman, after his arrival at Sardhana. These circumstances, added to my recollection of your uniform friendly conduct towards the British Government, and towards British subjects, render me desirous of promoting your comfort and

* Letter, dated Head-quarters, Muttra, 16 August, 1805, from Col. Malcolm, Civil Commissioner with H. E. the Rt. Hon. Lord Lake, to G. D. Guthrie Esq., Civil Commissioner deputed to H. H. the Begam Sombre's Camp. (*Refutation*, pp. 365-66).

satisfaction by every means in my power. I have reason to believe that the late Governor-General, aware of your attachment to the territory, which during so long a course of years has been in your possession, had it in contemplation to refrain from taking advantage of your consent to the transfer of your jagir. At all events, I have great pleasure in apprizing you, that reposing entire confidence in your disposition to maintain the obligations of attachment and fidelity to the British Government, *I have resolved to leave you in the unmolested possession of your jagir, with all the rights and privileges which you have hitherto enjoyed. As the condition of this indulgence, I have a right to expect that you will not only abstain from affording encouragement to those turbulent persons who are disposed to excite confusion and promote disorder, but that you will cordially assist in preventing their attempts to disturb the tranquillity of the Company's territories.*

I have directed Mr. Guthrie to proceed to Sardhana for the express purpose of communicating, in further detail, the sentiments and intentions expressed in this letter" (*Refutation*, pp. 363-64).

The Civil Commissioner, Mr. G. D. Guthrie, was deputed to the Begam and the final treaty or agreement with her was made in August 1805. Its terms were as follows:

> "Those places in the Doab which have formed the *jaidads* of Zeb-un-nisa Begam, shall remain to her as before from the Company as long as she may live. The troops of the Begam shall, according to custom, be always ready in the service of the East India Company. The Begam in every instance, considering herself a faithful friend of the Company, shall perform all the duties required from a friend, and shall not hold any intercourse whatever, either by agent or by letter, with any State or Power, or with the friends or dependents of any State or Power, or with the enemies or refractory subjects of the Company, or with any State or Power whatsoever but that of the Honourable the East India Company."—An agreement between George Dempster Guthrie Esq. on the part of the Hon. E. I. Co., and the Begam Sombre. (*Refutation*, p. 369).

She was reinvested with administrative powers over her province, and was left in "unmolested possession" with the rights and privileges she had formerly enjoyed.

Henceforth she maintained at her side only half of her troops, which were required for the protection of her person and the collection of the revenue, while the other half she had to depute for service with the English at her own expense.

APPENDIX *B*

FROM ZEB-UN-NISA BEGAM TO LORD WELLESLEY.
Dated (on the envelope) 4 Rabi-us-sani, 1217 H. =4 August 1802.

Received 9th September 1802.

After professions of submission and subserviency, and expressing an anxious desire of a personal interview, I have the honour to represent that, prior to this, I addressed a letter to the Honourable the Lt.-Governor, Mr. Wellesley,* on the subject of Colonel Collins's having taken his leave of the Maharajah Daulat Rao Sindhia and of Genl. Perron's having dismissed Col. Sutherland from his service which letter possibly may have come under your Lordship's inspection or the above intelligence may have reached your Lordship through the channel of the newspapers.

As Genl. Perron is aware of my being a well-wisher of the Company's Government and conceives that some of the *sardars* to the west are particularly well inclined towards me, he is night and day plotting confusion to my affairs, the subversion of my authority, and the accomplishment of my ruin. He wishes to annoy my troops in the same way that the Maharajah's army did formerly, though he has not yet succeeded in making any advances to effect this object, and I have introduced the same rules and

* Henry Wellesley (afterwards Lord Cowley) was appointed by his brother, Lord Wellesley, as Lt.-Governor of the newly acquired Ceded Districts.

regulations for the discipline of my battalions and artillery as exist under the Company's Government. But as the only child which I had, Zafar-yab Khan died some time ago, I have now no heir left to me in this world. I therefore desire that your Lordship, who at this auspicious season reflects lustre on the countries of Hindustan, would on the part of the Company take possession of all the property ordnance and stores whatsoever belonging to me, who am of the number of well-wishers and adherents of the Company. Whenever your Lordship may require them I am ready to give them up and if your Lordship pleases I will send a written instrument transferring them to the Company. Moreover at any time your Lordship may command my services, the performance of which I should consider as happiness both in my present and future life, I shall be prompt to obey. It is only with a view to the arrangement of this business that Hakim Mir Muhammad Jafar who is in my confidence and an inhabitant of the British territories remains in attendance on the Lt.-Governor at Bereilly. The Hakim will accordingly represent all particulars to your Lordship ; in your Lordship's answer to this *arzi* be pleased to communicate whatever may be proper and advisable to be done at the present season respecting this business, which will contribute to my honour, credit, and repose. Your Lordship will be pleased to communicate such further particulars as you deem necessary to the Lt.-Governor the Hon'ble Henry Wellesley. —*Vol. of Eng. Trans. of Pers. Letters Received*, 9-9-1802, No. 223 ; *Original Persian Letter* No. 323.

APPENDIX C

EXTRACT FROM A LETTER, DATED 15TH FEBY. 1805, FROM N. B. EDMONSTONE, SECY. TO GOVT., TO LT.-COL. OCHTERLONY, THE RESIDENT AT DELHI.

2. The information which H. E. the Governor-General has received from various quarters respecting the conduct of Begam Samru has satisfied H. E.'s mind that she has studiously endeavoured to maintain that species of temporizing policy which might induce Jaswant Rao Holkar to believe her to be attached to his cause, without proceeding to acts, which would place her in the condition of a public enemy to the British Power and might enable her to derive advantage from the success of either of the contending parties. This course of policy may be referred either to her concurrence in the extravagant supposition that success might ultimately attend the arms of Jaswant Rao Holkar against the British Power, or to her desire to avoid the danger, the loss or the expenses which might attend her actual co-operation with either party. Under the supposition that in the event of Holkar's success, she would retain the independent possession of her jagir in the Doab, she may justly be supposed to have desired his success, and this probable inclination of her mind justifies a suspicion that the report of her having fomented the disturbances in the Doab, is well founded, but the Governor-General is not apprized

of the existence of any positive evidence of that fact. The demonstration of that fact would augment the expediency of the immediate resumption of her territory in the Doab, and would deprive her of all title to an equivalent.

3. In the remarks to which the 1st paragraph of this dispatch refers, you appear to suggest the policy of confirming the Begam in the possession of her jagir during her life. This suggestion is founded on the extraordinary influence which she is supposed to possess over the Sikh chieftains and zamindars in that quarter and on her alleged disposition to favour the causes of the enemy.

5.......H. E. the Governor-General cannot concur in the expediency of the measure which you appear to recommend ; on the contrary, the speedy transfer of the Begam's jagir and her early removal with her troops from the Doab, must be considered to be urgent and necessary in the degree in which the Begam possesses the means of affecting the tranquillity of our possessions in that quarter by her political influence and local power. H. E. has accordingly determined to carry the arrangement into effect as soon as may be practicable.

6. The Governor-General does not desire that the Begam should be encouraged on any ground whatever, especially on the ground of her ability to injure or promote the British interests in her present situation, to expect the confirmation of her jagir which (as she has declared in her letter to the Governor-General, recd. 5th Dec. 1803) she has voluntarily consented to relinquish in exchange for

an equivalent on the right bank of the Jamuna. H. E. however wishes the Begam to understand that the exertion of her influence or the employment of her troops in the restoration of tranquillity and order in the northern quarter of the Doab will establish her claim to the same advantages in the nature or extent of her future tenure, beyond the limit of the existing agreement ; but that any act of treachery on her part will inevitably produce the destruction of her power and will absolve the British Government from the obligation to assigning to her any portion of territory on the right bank of the Jamuna after the resumption of her jagir in the Doab.

8. It may be proper to signify to you on this occasion that the British Govt. will be disposed to grant to the Begam compensation for the value of dwelling-houses or other property which she may relinquish on the transfer of her present jagir to the Hon'ble Company on an equitable valuation.

9. It seems probable that until H. E. the Commander-in-chief shall be enabled to detach a force into the Doab for the occupation of the territory to be resigned by the Begam, the arrangement with the Begam cannot conveniently be carried into effect. Under any circumstances, however, the Governor-General deems it extremely desirable to a right understanding with the Begam without delay and you will accordingly proceed to make the necessary communications as soon as you shall be authorized by the Commander-in-chief to that effect.

10. If any exigency should exist to require an alteration of the former propositions to the Begam, the

Commander-in-chief will exercise his judgment upon that state of affairs ; and in such a crisis, if H. E. should deem it to be advisable, he will authorize you to signify to the Begam the intention of the British Govt. to confirm her present jagir in the Doab to her for the period of her life. In this case, however, it will be necessary to stipulate for the reduction of her force, or for the removal of her French officers, and the substitution of British officers in their place. The total reduction of her brigades would be the most advisable measure, accompanied by an agreement to subsidize whatever the Commander-in-chief might deem to be the necessary proportion within the Doab. If however the Commander-in-chief should not perceive any necessity of yielding to the Begam's change of sentiments respecting the transfer of her jagir, it would be a far preferable arrangement to remove her establishment to the right bank of the Jamuna, and even in this case, it would be proper to endeavour to accomplish a total reduction of regular corps, and the dismission of her French officers together with subsidiary alliance founded on the principles stated in this paragraph.

Secret Procdgs. 28-3-1805, No. 157.

CHAPTER VII

LATTER DAYS OF BEGAM SAMRU

Her treaty of August 1805 with the British Government marks the end of Begam Samru's political career. Henceforth her power was limited to her own jagir, where she continued to be absolute.

She now turned her attention entirely to the improvement of her State and the welfare of her subjects. Her first anxiety was for those of her dependents who might be rendered helpless by her death. She, therefore, thought it imperative that some provision should be made, after her death, for those "who attached themselves to her fortunes, at a time when her situation was precarious, and from their being the relatives of those who have fallen in her service, and the loss of whom deprives them of all support but what must be derived from her; and as some of them have been accustomed to comfort, and even to affluence, their distress, if left in a destitute state, would be the more severely felt."* She was well advanced in years, and was naturally afraid that her wishes might not be realized at all if she delayed longer in giving effect to them. So, she wrote in July 1807 to Sir George Barlow, the then Governor-General, soliciting the assurance of a provision amounting to a monthly sum of 7,500 Sicca† Rupees in favour of certain of her dependents after her death.

As it was the close of Sir George Barlow's tenure of office, he could not himself do anything for the Begam, but he recommended her letter to his successor, Lord Minto, who, "deeming this application to be in all respects just and reasonable, and the general tenor of her conduct to merit every practicable degree of favour and indulgence on the part of the British Government, was graciously pleased to comply with her request."‡

---

* Letter dated 9-7-1807 from the Resident at Delhi to the Secretary to Government. (*Refutation*, p. 403).

† Calcutta Sicca Rupee—176 gr. of pure silver plus 16 gr. alloy; weight 192 gr. or 1·0666 tolas. Farrukhabad Sonat Rupee—165 gr. of pure silver plus 15 gr. alloy; weight 180 gr. or 1 tola. One Sicca Rupee is therefore equal to Re. 1-1-1 of the present currency.

‡ The Begam was requested to transmit to Government a detailed statement of the names of the persons for whom

The following letter was accordingly addressed by Minto to the Begam on 4th August, 1807 :—

"All the circumstances of your situation, and of your uniform attachment and fidelity to the British Government are well known to me, and I avail myself with satisfaction of the present opportunity of expressing those sentiments of respect and regard which the distinguished merit of your character and conduct have justly excited in my mind.... The solicitude which you have manifested for the future welfare of your dependents is consistent with that spirit of liberality and justice which distinguishes your character, and has hitherto rendered them the objects of your bounty. I have great satisfaction in communicating to you my compliance with your wishes as described in your letter to Mr. Seton" (*Refutation*, pp. 406-7).

Being thus greatly relieved from anxiety as to the future welfare of her dependents and relatives, the Begam, who had in early life embraced the Catholic religion, now "devoted herself to its maintenance with earnestness and

---

she had solicited a provision, and of the amount to be apportioned to each out of the promised sum of 7,500 Sicca Rupees a month, but no list appears to have been submitted during her lifetime.

zeal. By her own exemplary conduct, and laudable encouragement, a considerable congregation of native Christians, reckoned at two thousand souls at least, was settled about her at Sardhana. In her house the Capuchin Fathers of the Tibetan Mission found a home, and every opportunity of discharging their duties; but owing to the continual moving about, which her position and duty rendered inevitable, there was no proper church set apart for worship" (*Sardhana*, p. 42). In 1820 she had a grand church built at Sardhana after the model of St. Peter's at Rome. This building is "said to be the finest without any exception in India", and cost four *lakhs* of Rupees. In 1822 it was first opened for public worship and was consecrated by the Prefect Apostolic of Agra, the Rev. Fr. Antoninus Pezzoni. This gigantic pile was named the Cathedral Church of St. Mary and testifies to the Begam's incomparable attachment to her religion. She built a chapel, which was named St. Paul's in 1830, for the Rev. Mr. Richards, the Church Missionary at Meerut, "at a cost of Rs. 10,000" (Sleeman, ii. 287) to meet the wants of the Indian Protestants. This was commonly known as the Hindustani Chapel, and was the only church, erected by her for religious purposes, left without any allowance. It exists to this day in the Meerut Cantonment. Since 1st July, 1892 it has been used by the Chaplain of Meerut as a parochial school, which is at present known as St. John's School.* The beautiful chapel in Meerut Cantonment, which is known as St. Joseph's Catholic Church, was also built by her in 1834† for the use of the British Catholic soldiers. It was

---

* I am indebted to Miss B. S. Murphy, the Head Mistress of St. John's School, for consulting old records and supplying me with the dates of the erection of the chapel and the installation of the school.

We also learn from the *N.-W. P. Gaz.* (iii. 409) "that the expense in building the Meerut Church—begun in 1819 and completed in 1821—was partly defrayed by subscription and partly by a grant from Government, and amongst the subscribers was Begam Samru." On reference to the C.M.S., Meerut, I have been informed by the Rev. L. C. Perfume that the church referred to here is the Church of St. John the Baptist, in Meerut Cantonment, built for the European soldiers and civilians.

† The date of erection of this church, which has since been enlarged and remodelled, has been supplied to me from records by the Catholic Chaplain, Rev. Fr. Sylvester, O. C., to whom my cordial thanks are due.

then in charge of Padre McDonald, who used to get an allowance of Rs. 100 per mensem from the Begam.

Shortly before her death the Begam succeeded in making arrangements for the disposition of her property. By her will, executed on 16th December 1831,* she made David Ochterlony Dyce and Clemence Brown, a Colonel of the Bengal Artillery, her executors. Her Highness, however, did not think the will which was in the English language sufficient. She, therefore, on 17th December 1834, invited over to her palace at Sardhana the Magistrate of Meerut, and several of the principal military officers and European residents of that station for the purpose of attesting a deed of gift,† which she had

---

* The latter part of the will is given on pages 373-75 of Dyce Sombre's *Refutation*. A copy of the entire will is now among the records of the Panjab Civil Secretariat. In an attested copy of it—kindly supplied to me by the Chief Secretary to the Govt. of the Panjab, the date of the document is by mistake given as 16th Dec. 1830, instead of 16th December *1831*. Attached to the original will were four engagements or wills, written in English, giving particulars for the division of 3,57,000 Sicca Kaldar Farrukhabad Rupees, but these I have not yet been able to trace.

† This legal instrument, drawn up in Persian, ratified the contents of the previous testament in English. For an English translation of the deed of gift, *Refutation*, pp. 376-79.

prepared in Persian—a language familiar to her—and in the presence of all divested herself of her personal property of every description in favour of her adopted son David. From that day David Dyce had to identify himself as one of the family of Sombre, and took the name of David Ochterlony Dyce Sombre.

After the execution of the will in December 1831, she entrusted the entire management of her State to her adopted son, and devoted herself exclusively to religion and charity. Referring to her gifts and donations her contemporary, Bacon, writes:—"She is, as a public character, notoriously generous, when called upon to loosen her purse-strings, distributing freely to the indigent, and in no instance refusing her aid in the construction or benefit of any public institution." But, to mention a special trait of her character, "in smaller matters, she was not so open-handed, and no fractional expenditure was permitted in her establishment without her own immediate approval; even the common disbursements of her household were inspected and examined personally" (Bacon, ii. 47).

On 12th January 1834 Begam Samru, "as a small token of her sincere love for the Holy Religion she professed," sent to Gregory XVI, the Pope of Rome, a lakh and a half of Sonat Rupees, equivalent to £13,704-3s.-4d., to make such charitable use of it as he might think fit. An Italian priest from Milan named Fr. Julius Cæsar (Scotti) was her domestic chaplain. To mark her appreciation of the Father, she recommended him to the Pope for the Bishopric of Sardhana, and asked for a decoration for her adopted son, Dyce Sombre. Her last prayer was for the fatherly benediction of His Holiness for her eternal welfare and a relic for her church. Fr. Julius Cæsar was raised to the episcopal dignity, under the title of Bishop of Amathunta *in partibus infidelium*, and Dyce Sombre was made a Chevalier of the Order of Christ. At the same time she remitted to the Archbishop of Canterbury, as head of the Church of England, fifty thousand Sonat Rupees (£4,580-16s.-8d.) the interest on which was to be distributed annually among a number of the most deserving Protestant charitable institutions in England.

By a deed of gift* dated 18th February 1834, the Begam contributed a lakh and a half of Sonat Rupees to the Church of England, which was invested under the name of the *Begam Samru Trust* in Calcutta. This trust is administered by the Lord Bishop and Archdeacon of Calcutta. Two funds were established with the money:—

(*a*) CLERGY FUND. A sum of one *lakh* of Sonat (95,600 Sicca) Rupees was settled on this fund in Government Paper. The object of the fund is to "provide instruction and maintenance for a number of young men in order to make them eligible for ordination according to the rites and requisites of the Protestant Episcopal Church."

(*b*) POOR FUND. The balance of fifty thousand Sonat (47,800 Sicca) Rupees was given to this fund as principal in Government Paper. Many needy and neccessitous persons living in Calcutta or its suburbs

---

* A copy of this deed is reproduced in full on pages 3-21 in Archdeacon J. H. Pratt's *Some Account of Endowments and Institutions in connexion with the Diocese and Archdeaconry of Calcutta* (Cal. 1865). My best thanks are due to the Lord Bishop of Calcutta for allowing me access to this rare book.

were occasionally sent to jails for very small debts. It was a condition of the trust to have the deserving debtors liberated on Good Friday in each year out of the income of the fund during the lifetime of the Begam and, after her demise, on the anniversary of her death. Should there be no objects of charity in this direction the whole of the interest accrued would have to be distributed among the poor and necessitous persons in Calcutta or in its suburbs.

The trustees of the Begam Samru Trust are authorized to spend only the interest accruing from the principal amounts.*

Shortly before her death the Begam formed a wish to endow the religious and charitable institutions she had founded

---

* We quote an extract from the *Christian Intelligencer* (reprinted in the *Friend of India* of the 8th March, 1838, pp. 90-91) concerning the administration of the Begam Samru Trust :—

"BEGAM SOMBRE'S FUND.—On 31st January [1838] last, the Lord Bishop and the Archdeacon distributed Rs. 2,000 from this fund to the most necessitous poor in Calcutta, and relieved thirty-four individuals from imprisonment for small debts. The portion of this fund devoted to missionary purposes, yields about Rs. 400 monthly. It is devoted at present to the maintenance of a native missionary, and of several natives preparing for instructors to their countrymen at Bishop's College."

during her lifetime. For this purpose she set aside some monies, and Mr. Dyce Sombre, her adopted son and heir, carried her intentions into effect after her death by means of trust deeds:

(1) The interest on a *lakh* of Sonat (95,600 Sicca) Rupees in Promissory Note of the E. I. Co. for the use and purpose of keeping in proper repair the Church of St. Mary at Sardhana and of paying to the offg. Bishop or priest of the said church, or, in case of there being no such Bishop or priest, to the offg. priest nearest to Sardhana, the sum of Rs. 15 per week for prayers for the repose of the soul of the late Begam; and further of paying to the offg. Bishop or priest of the said church such reasonable salary as to the trustees may seem fit; and lastly of paying the residue, if any, towards the relief of such persons resident at Sardhana or in its vicinity as may appear to the trustees fit objects of charity. —*Indenture* dated 3-10-1836. [This fund had an annual income of Rs. 4,000].

(2) The interest on a *lakh* of Sonat (95,600 Sicca) Rupees for the support of the Roman Catholic College [St. John's College] in the town of Sardhana, the object of which was to train up native Christians as Catholic missionaries; failing that, for the use and purpose of some other charitable

object and purpose within the town of Sardhana and not elsewhere.—*Indenture* dated 15-2-1838 executed by Solaroli on behalf of Dyce Sombre. [The annual income of this fund amounted to Rs. 4,000].

(3) The interest on fifty thousand Sonat (47,800 Sicca) Rupees for the benefit of such indigent persons in the district of Sardhana as were supported by the Begam in her lifetime, and the surplus, if any, for other indigent persons residing in the same district, preference being given to persons of the Christian religion.—*Indenture* dated 3-10-1836. [The annual income of this fund was Rs. 2,000].

(4) To the Catholic Chapel at Meerut, built by Her Highness, the interest on twelve thousand and five hundred Sicca (13,000 Sonat) Rupees. The object of this trust is to reserve a sufficient sum out of the income [about Rs. 520 annually] for necessary repairs and to pay the residue towards the support of the offg. priest, or if there shall be no such priest at the said chapel or if by any other reason there shall in the course of time be any surplus of the said interest, then it shall be lawful for the trustees to dispose of such surplus towards the relief and support of indigent persons residing in and about the station of Meerut.*—*Indenture* dated 3-10-1836.

* The interest on this fund is at present expended by the priest in helping the poor and needy residing in or near

(5) To the Roman Catholic Chapel at Agra, erected by Her Highness, the interest on twenty-eight thousand, seven hundred Sicca (30,000 Sonat) Rupees. The income [annually Rs. 1,200] is expended on the maintenance of the chapel, and on charity to the needy in and about the station of Agra.—*Indenture* dated 11-11-1836.

(6) To the Roman Catholic churches at Calcutta, Bombay and Madras the interest on 32,000, 31,800, and 31,800 Sicca Rupees respectively, aggregating one *lakh* of Sonat Rupees.*

Though a considerable portion of her money was given away for the spread of

---

Meerut, as the Government took over the Meerut Chapel over 60 years ago, since when it has been repaired and kept up by the P. W. D. as a Govt. building.

* Owing to the principal trustee—Mr. Dyce Sombre—having gone out of his mind, and his subsequent death, the trust notes were practically held by the Bishop of Agra and interest drawn by him until 1871, when Col. T. B. Butt, the Agent of the Sardhana palace (owned by the late Lady Forester, Dyce Sombre's heir) moved the local Government to reconstitute these trusts—*vide* his letter No. 590 dated 11th Feby. 1871 to the Secy. to Govt. N.-W. P., after which nothing further appears to have been done until 1892-3 when the Legal Remembrancer to the local Govt. moved the High Court of the N.-W. P. to reconstitute these trusts, and to appoint trustees. This was done at the instance of the late Lady Forester (vice Dyce Sombre) in her capacity as his legal representative, and heir-at-law.

In 1892-3 the High Court carried out the Legal Remembrancer's request by framing the following trust deeds,

Christianity, the Begam showed a remarkable catholicity of views. She subscribed liberally "towards Hindu and Musalman institutions also" (*N.-W. P. Gaz.* iii. 295). She also contributed largely towards the construction of bridges and similar works of utility to the general public.

The shades of evening were gathering fast on her long and eminently active life. She had an attack of fever and "after a few days' illness, during which she retained her consciousness to the last, prepared by the sacrament and prayers of the church, she quietly expired" at Sardhana

---

appointing trustees, and vesting the endowment fund of each trust :—

Sardhana	College	End. Fund	Rs.	101,900	Company's Rs.
Do.	Church	do.	,,	101,900	do.
Do.	Poor	do.	,,	50,900	do.

The above monies are invested in Govt. 3½% Securities of 1865, which are in the custody of the Meerut Treasury, as ordered by the High Court in the trust deeds, and the interest is drawn to meet the expenses of the respective trusts.

I take this opportunity of conveying my warmest thanks to Mr. E. C. Roberts—a mutiny veteran—who now holds the office of Secretary, Sardhana Charitable Trusts, for allowing me access to a copy of Col. Butt's above-mentioned letter (with annexures, including copies of the trust deeds of the Agra and Meerut Chapels) as well as to copies of the trust deeds of 1836 and 1892-3 relating to the Church, College, and the Poor.

about half-past six in the morning of Wednesday, the 27th January 1836.

It is said that a saint, Shakir Shah, had foretold the date of her death. This saint used to live at Meerut. One day there arose in his mind a sudden desire to go to Sardhana, "where he found the old lady very dangerously ill and not expected to live. He himself was very old and ill when he set out from Meerut; and the journey is said to have shaken him so much that he found his end approaching, and sent a messenger to the princess with these words: *Aya tore, chalé ham*; that is, 'Death came for thee, but I go in thy place'; and he told those around him that she had precisely five years more to live. She is said to have caused a tomb to be built over him, and is believed by the people to have died that day five years" (Sleeman, ii. 237).

Everything remained perfectly tranquil for the rest of the day. At 9 o'clock at night her body was removed from the inner apartments to lie in state in the hall, and there it remained until 8 o'clock on the following morning, when it was deposited in the coffin.

"At nine, the whole of the arrangements being completed, the body was carried out, borne by the native Christians of the artillery battalion, under a canopy, supported by the principal officers of her late Highness's troops, and the pall by Messrs. Dyce Sombre, Solaroli, Drever, and Troup, preceded by the whole of Her Highness's body-guards, followed by the Bishop, chaunting portions of the service, aided by the choristers of the cathedral. After them, the Magistrate, Mr. Hamilton, and then the chief officers of the household, the whole brought up by a battalion of her late Highness's infantry, and a troop of horse. The procession, preceded by four elephants from which alms and cakes were distributed amongst the crowd, passed through a street formed of the troops at Sardhana, to the door of the cathedral, the entrance to which was kept by a guard of honour from the 30th N. I., under the command of Capt. Campbell. The procession passed into the body of the cathedral, in the centre of which the coffin was deposited on tressels. High mass was then performed in excellent style, and with great feeling, by the Bishop. The body was lowered into the vault" (*Meerut Observer*).

The following extract from the *Meerut Observer* of the time graphically describes the scenes that followed the announcement of her death and illustrates how that event affected her subjects and dependents alike :—

> "The crowds assembled outside the palace-walls, and on the roads, were immense, and one scene of lamentation and sorrow was apparent ; the grief was deep and silent ; the clustered groups talked of nothing but the heavy loss they had sustained, and the intensity of their sorrow was pictured in their countenances, nor did they separate during the night. According to the custom of the country, the whole of the dependents observed a strict fast ; there was no preparing of meals, no retiring to rest ; all were watchful, and every house was a scene of mourning. . . . .
>
> Thus terminated the career of one who, for upwards of half-a-century, had held a conspicuous place in the political proceedings of India. In the Begam Samru the British authorities had an ardent and sincere ally, ever ready, in the spirit of true chivalry, to aid and assist, to the utmost of her means, their fortunes and interests."

Immediately after her death, Dr. Drever, the physician to Her Highness, had despatched the news of the event to the Magistrate of Meerut, Mr. R. N. C. Hamilton, who, accompanied by the

Commissioner, Mr. J. R. Hutchinson, arrived at Sardhana at about 12 o'clock noon on that very day.

When the burial service was over, the relatives of the Begam as also the Magistrate, retired into the palace. A proclamation was then read in the presence of the Magistrate, announcing the annexation of her *jagir* by the British Government and making it subject to the regulations in force in the territories under the Company.* The authority of the Begam's

---

* Dyce Sombre, on the day following her death, handed over to the Magistrate of Meerut, for transmission to the proper authorities, a list of the persons which, he mentioned, was drawn out agreeably to the Begam's instructions, and in a memorial sent on 1st June, 1837, to Lord Auckland, the then Governor-General of India, (*Pol. Con.* 12-6-1837, No. 69) he prayed that his Lordship would be graciously pleased to grant the pensions mentioned in the list prepared by her late Highness. His father, Col. G.A.D. Dyce—who lost the Begam's favour on account of his conduct—also submitted to the British Government the counterpart of a pension list (*Pol. Procdgs.* 22 Aug. 1836, No. 34) which, he alleged, the Begam had forwarded in 1807 to Mr. Seton, the Resident at Delhi. The British Government held that the list of persons on whom she desired pensions to be conferred, not being duly authenticated, was not binding on them. The Governor-General, however, concurring in the view taken by the Lt.-Governor, N.-W.P., sanctioned in his letter, dated 26-9-1836, (*Pol. Con.* 26-9-1836, No. 42) the grant of life-pensions to the extent of Rs. 1,483-9-6 a month

officers having ceased with her death, her estate came under the sole management of the English officers, whose orders alone were to be obeyed. Proclamations were accordingly made that day at the

---

to 668 persons who were left in a state of destitution. This pension was granted on the basis of a pension list (*Pol. Con.* 26-9-1836, No. 41) showing a total of Rs. 5,910-13-9, but on a reduced scale, as many of the persons on this list were not considered to have any claim on the British Govt. The pension list alluded to here, which was obtained by the Meerut Magistrate, "was drawn out from the records of the late Begam's Pay Office and had been compared with the list of pensions actually paid or called over when the arrears were adjusted in Feby. 1836," *i.e.*, the month following the Begam's death.

Dyce Sombre, grieved at the miserable circumstances in which many of the dependents of the late Begam were placed, was therefore obliged "to pension them out of his own private income to the amount of nearly £2,000 [about Rs. 20,000] per annum" (*Refutation*, p. 437*n*). However, on 15th July, 1839, he again placed this matter before the Chairman and Directors of the E. I. Co., praying that "the Hon'ble Court would see the justice of granting the amount specified, *viz.* Rs. 7,500 monthly,...............divided proportionately amongst the oldest of the Begam's adherents, as it would be borne in mind that out of nearly 8,000 public servants, some of them of 50 years' standing, a small number only were in receipt of pensions to the aggregate amount of Rs. 1,500 monthly" (*Refutation*, p. 441). This memorial was not without its effect, as the Government found it necessary "to grant an increase of about Rs. 500 a year [? month] more, making a total of Rs. 2,000, while the Government had bound itself to give £9,000 a year, or a monthly allowance of Rs. 7,500" (*Ibid.* p. 446*n*).

principal towns in the different parts of the *jagir*.

Thereafter the Magistrate, in the presence of the Begam's relations and principal officers, read the will executed by her in respect of her personal property* which, "amounting to nearly half a *krore*, devolved upon Mr. Dyce Sombre, with the exception of small legacies and charitable bequests" (*Meerut Observer*).

---

* The letter addressed by the Magistrate on 28th January, 1836 to the Commissioner gives a graphic account of the proceedings after the Begam's death. See *Pol. Con.* 22-2-1836, No. 26.

CHAPTER VIII

BEGAM SAMRU'S POSSESSIONS

Jagir

Begam Samru was not a sovereign princess; her status was that of a jagirdar holding lands of the Delhi crown on military tenure, *i.e.*, she was granted a certain district of which she enjoyed the public revenue under the obligation of maintaining a body of troops, to be employed, when called upon, by her sovereign. Her jagir lay in the Gangetic Doab and stretched from Muzaffarnagar to Aligarh, including within its area the *parganas* of Sardhana, Karnal, Budhana, Barnawa, Baraut, Kutana, Tappal, and Jewar. (*Refutation*, p. 372). The principal *pargana* of this *jagir* and the seat of its administration was Sardhana.

The Begam's "estate was extremely wealthy and well provided with fine towns such as Baraut, Dinauli, Barnawa, Sardhana, Jewar and Dankaur, and close by her dominions were the large marts of

Meerut, Shamli, Kandhla, Bágpat,...... Shahdara, and Delhi" (*N.-W. P. Gaz.* iii. 295).

She had some trans-Jamuna estates too, which she claimed as her *altamgha* or royal grant in perpetuity. Among her properties in this region may be mentioned the *pargana* of Badshapur-Jharsa, consisting of "about 70 villages, distant about 14 miles from Delhi" (*Refutation*, p. 448). Bhutgong, a village in *pargana* Sonipat, and the "*mauza* of Bhogipura-Shahganj and a garden in *subah* Akbarabad [Agra]"* were also held by her as personal property.

Her right of possession was confirmed during the successive administrations of

* We learn from a letter of the Begam to the Governor-General that the "garden of Shahganj and the village of Bhogipura, yielding a small revenue, in the neighbourhood of Agra were, from the time of Monsr. Samru, bestowed on Nawab Zafar-yab Khan for his expenses" (*Pol. Procdgs.* 29-10-1832, No. 71). Maharajah Madho Narayan, the Peshwa, granted these lands in *jagir* to the Begam, under a *sanad* dated 2 Shawwal 1205 H.=5 June 1791. (*Ibid.* No. 72; *Refutation*, pp. 372-73, 383).

Shahganj, a suburb of Agra, exactly two miles west of Agra fort, on the road from Agra to Fathpur-Sikri. A little further on the same road, the walled garden of Begam Samru was standing as late as the mutiny.

Mirza Najaf Khan, Mirza Shafi, and Afrasiab Khan, and when Mahadji Sindhia became supreme at Delhi, he "added to the extent of them by a grant of some other lands south-west of the Jamuna" (*Shah-Aulum*, p. 148). Daulat Rao Sindhia, who succeeded Mahadji in February, 1794, also "confirmed the Begam's right and title to her jagir, as well as to her landed possessions which were of a personal character" (*Refutation*, pp. 372-73), and entrusted to her charge the defence of his western frontier against the incursions of the Sikhs. "Her wages as a partizan were fixed lastly by Sindhia [Daulat Rao?] at 50 thousand Rupees by the month, or six *lakhs* a year; the payment of that allowance was fixed on eight provinces or *parganas* which had been delivered for the purpose of receiving it."*

The extent of the Begam's *jagir* varied from time to time. Bala Bai, daughter of Mahadji Sindhia, once held several villages in the Meerut district, which were sequestered when hostilities

* Letter, dated 2-4-1795, from Col. Levassoult to Lt.-Col. M'Gowan.—*Refutation*, pp. 443-44.

broke out between the British and Sindhia in 1803. Nine of her villages, *viz.*, Kahwai, Hara, Bijwára, Phusar, Halwari, Alawalpur, Bitáoda, Barauda and Mindkali—were situated in the *parganas* of Barnawa and Budhana in the heart of Begam Samru's territory, and of these the Begam was placed in temporary charge. But she could not enjoy their revenue long, as Bala Bai's jagir was restored by the 7th article of the treaty of Sarji Anjangaon* (30th December 1803). The Begam, therefore, was obliged to relinquish the villages in question (about July 1804) in compliance with a request made by the Resident at Delhi. On the death of Bala Bai (*circa* August 1833), Her Highness wrote to the Governor-General, Lord William Bentinck, on 6th January, 1834 for the restoration of these villages on the plea that they "were formerly in her possession, and the only just claim upon them was hers, as feudal sovereign."†
But her claim was disallowed.

---

* Aitchison's *Treaties, Engagements & Sanads*, iv. 43. *Pol. Procdgs.* 11 Aug. 1810, No. 31.

† *Pol. Cons.* 29 Jany. 1834, Nos. 20-21.

The *pargana* of Pahasu in the Doab, "containing 54 villages" (*N.-W. P. Gaz.* iii. 169) was granted to her by Daulat Rao Sindhia in 1803; at the battle of Assaye (23 Sep. 1803) she rendered military help to her overlord, Sindhia, by despatching five of her battalions to fight under his flag. "Agreeably to her contract with Sindhia she was bound to furnish him with three battalions and 12 guns, at her own expense. When these battalions used to march to the Deccan they received from Sindhia an *extra* allowance of pay, which commenced from the time they crossed the Chambal, and ceased on the day they recrossed that river on their return. Three battalions marched to the Deccan, and these were followed by two more."* As the last two battalions were in excess of the contingent to be furnished by the Begam according to stipulation, Sindhia granted the revenues of the districts of Pahasu and Murthal to discharge

---

* Letter, dated Septr. 1805, from G. D. Guthrie, Collector of Saharanpur to Col. J. Malcolm, Resident etc. Hd.-qrs., Muttra. *Secret Con.* 21-11-1805, No. 53.

their pay.* Genl. Perron gave up Pahasu to her, but would not relinquish Murthal.

Her *jagir* was the most valuable in the Doab, possessing as it did, the advantages of the Canal, the Jamuna and Hindun rivers, the Krishni and Kali nadis, which afforded an ample supply of water; and the soil, being naturally fertile, produced an abundance of grain of all kinds, cotton, sugar-cane, and tobacco. The cultivators in her territory "were mostly Jats, well known to be the best cultivators and payers of revenue in India; their industry and superior husbandry enabling them to make a far more respectable appearance than any other class."

Revenue

With the death of the Begam her *jagir* lapsed to the British Government. "The portions of the Samru estates included

---

* "Daulat Rao......gave me the *parganas* of Murthal and Pahasu in *jaidad,* and I received from him *sanads* for several districts Ramaund [Ranod?] among others which produce a revenue of several *lakhs* of Rupees."—Begam to Lt.-Col. Ochterlony dated 3-2-1804. *Sect. Procdgs.* 2-3-1804, No. 252; *Pol. Procdgs.* 6-2-1834, No. 43.

in the Meerut district on its lapse...... comprised *parganas* Sardhana, Budhana, Baraut, Kutáná and Barnáwa, and two other villages... The net demand of all these parganas for twenty years (1814-1834 A.D.) averaged Rs. 5,86,650, including cesses, while the collections during the same period averaged Rs. 5,67,211 with balances, amounting on the whole to only Rs. 19,439" (*N.-W. P. Gaz.* iii. 431).

From a passage in a memorial sent to the Government by Dyce Sombre, the Begam's heir, we find that the "territories within the Doab in the Upper Hindustan yielded a revenue of eight *lakhs* of Rupees per annum" (*Refutation*, p. 427). We have shown above that the yearly income from only a portion of the Begam's *jagir* in the Doab was about 6 *lakhs* of Rupees, and it is not unlikely that the remaining parganas brought in another two *lakhs*.

The annual income from *pargana* Badshapur-Jharsa, outside the Doab, amounted to "about 82 thousand Rupees; from the village of Bhutgong 22 thousand, and from other villages [*mauza* Bhogipura-Shahganj?] 8 thousand." Approximately her income from these places amounted to a *lakh*. (*Refutation*, pp. 171, 347*n*, 352).

Some of the correspondence between the Begam and the Company helps us in forming an estimate of certain other sources of her income. For instance, we learn that the Begam enjoyed the right to collect transit duties on goods passing through her territories by land and water.*

The average annual collection of river duties from the parganas of Jewar and Tappal in five years amounted to Rs. 3,305-8-7 and that of land transit duties to Rs. 3,711-5-3.

River duties were collected from the ghats in the parganas of Jewar, Tappal, and Kutana only. There were no ghats

---

* The extent of the net receipts from these duties during the 5 years—1242-1246 H. (1826-27 to 1830-31)—after deducting the pay of the collecting officers and pensions, was shown in the Abstract Statement (*Pol. Con.* 18-6-1832, No. 87) compiled by Her Highness's *wakil*, Muhammad Rahamat Khan, and submitted to the Government in May, 1832. The figures are as follows :—

H. 1242-1246	Land Duties	Water Duties
Pargana Jewar ...	Rs. 8,719-15-0	Rs. 10,062-8-0
,, Tappal ...	,, 9,836-11-3	,, 6,465-3-0
	Rs. 18,556-10-3	Rs. 16,527-11-0

in any of the other districts belonging to the Begam at which water duties were levied. In September 1832, she came to an arrangement with the British Government whereby "she agreed to accept in half-yearly instalments the sum of Rs. 4,466-12-6,* to be paid from the Delhi treasury, in commutation of her right to collect duties at all her ghats on the Jamuna both above and below Delhi.†

The Begam's right to the transit duties on land was never interfered with. In those days good metalled roads were rare and the only road, properly so called, frequented by the traders was the one from Meerut to Sardhana, and for the use of this road she levied duty on the passing merchandise. In addition to this, she had other sources of income, though small, in the form of petty imposts on "village markets and fairs, and also fees

---

* Rs. 3,644-3-11 for the ghats of the two *parganas* of Jewar and Tappal, and Rs. 822-8-7 for those of Kutana.—Letter, dated 31-8-1832, from W. Fraser, Agent to the Govr.-Genl. to the Secretary to the Govr.-Genl. *Pol. Con.* 8 Octr. 1832, No. 10.

† Letter, dated 12-9-1832 from W. H. Macnaghten, Secy. to the Govr.-Genl., to the Chief Secy. to Govt., Fort Wm.—*Pol. Con.* 8 Octr. 1832, No. 9.

from pilgrims to shrines" (*Meerut Universal Magazine*, 1837, iv. 276).

Her Expenditure

Her military establishment (according to Sleeman) "cost her about four *lakhs* of Rupees a year; her civil establishments eighty thousand, and her household establishments and expenses about the same—total six *lakhs* of Rupees a year. The revenue of Sardhana and the other lands assigned at different times for the payment of the force has been at no time more than sufficient to cover these expenses" (ii. 284).

These observations appear to be true, for the maintenance of very extensive establishments and other heavy expenses did not admit of her "bequeathing in cash more than about half-a-*krore* of Rupees" (*Pol. Con.* 22-8-1836, No. 34). Leaving aside the larger items, even the pensions which she paid to her dependents amounted to Rs. 5,910-13-9 a month. Since her treaty with the British she enjoyed for three entire decades the undisturbed possession of her territories, and some are inclined to think that if she had wished it, she might have laid by a far greater amount in cash than she actually left behind her. But this seems to be a wrong estimate, as her treaty with the British did not permit of her expenses —in particular the military expenditure —being curtailed to any appreciable extent. She had to bear the necessary charges even for that half of her troops, *viz.*, 3 battalions and a park of artillery, which was, according to the terms of the treaty, always employed in the Company's service.

Army

As a jagirdar of the Emperor of Delhi the Begam had to maintain an army to help her sovereign in his need. "Part of her army resided at Sardhana, her capital, and part at Delhi, in attendance upon the Emperor" (Sleeman, ii. 277). Apart from her regular army, she raised irregular troops (*sehbandi*) whenever need arose. She had a well-stored arsenal and a foundry for cannon within the walls of a small fortress built near her dwelling at Sardhana. Her army was a well-disciplined force, composed of infantry, artillery and a complement of cavalry, led by Europeans of different nationalities, like Marchand, Baours, Evans, and Dudrenec, who, after the murder of the German General Pauli in 1782, were principally occupied in opposing the inroads of the Sikhs. After them the command of her troops devolved successively upon George Thomas, Levassoult, Saleur, Pœthod and John Renny Sabia. "At the time of her death her forces were led by Genl. Reghalini and eleven other European officers, one of whom was John Thomas, son of the celebrated George Thomas" (*N.-W. P. Gaz.* iii. 295).

The Begam was herself a fearless warrior and a clever leader of troops. She commanded her army on many a battle-field, and "Col. Skinner had often, during his service with the Marathas, seen her, then a beautiful young woman, leading on her troops to the attack in person, and displaying in the midst of the most frightful carnage, the greatest intrepidity and presence of mind" (Beale, 251; *As. Journal*, 1834, Sep.-Dec., p. 146). "The people in the Deccan, who knew the Begam by reputation, believed her to be a witch, who destroyed her enemies by throwing her *chadir* at them; the word meaning 'chain-shot' as well as a 'woman's veil'" (Skinner, i. 286*n*). After her treaty with the British she was never found on the battle-field again, except on one occasion. The siege of Bharatpur, conducted by Lord Combermere, revived all her military ardour, and she was desirous of taking the field and obtaining a share of the glory. Major Archer, Aide-de-camp to Lord Combermere, writes:

> "When the army was before Bharatpur, in 1826, the Commander-in-chief was desirous that no Native chief of our allies should accompany the besieging force with any of his troops; this order hurt the pride of the Begam, who remonstrated. She was told that the large and holy place of Muttra was to be confided to her care. 'Nonsense, said she, 'if I don't go to Bharatpur, all Hindustan will say I am grown a coward in my old age'" (i 144*n*).

Mrs. Deane, a British officer's wife who visited Sardhana about 1810, has left the following very interesting description of her soldiers:—

> "We were escorted over the estate by her colonel commandant, a respectable old gentleman of

> the name of Peton, a Frenchman by birth, but resident at her Court for many years. She has a regular cantonment here for her troops, and a strong fort containing some good houses, which are inhabited by the officers and their families. Her soldiers are tall, stout men, with light complexions, hooked noses, and strongly marked features, being principally Rajputs, who are the best soldiers, but much addicted to chewing opium, generally proud, and often insolent. Their uniform is a dress of dark blue broad cloth, reaching to the feet, with scarlet turbans and waistbands. Her park of artillery seemed also in excellent order: most of the large guns stood in a line in front of the palace gates" (p. 149).

Bacon speaks of the dresses of her military officers as "the most heterogeneous and varied possible, being worn according to the taste or fancy of each, without regard to uniformity of pattern or colour; but the troops are clad in vests of dark yellow cloth, with some attention to conformity of cut, and they are all armed and appointed alike. They are not very military in appearance, but are said to be good soldiers, both in courage and hardihood" (ii. 53).

The strength of her army varied at

different times, and we learn from the *Ibratnama* (iii. 26) that in 1787 when the Begam discomfitted Ghulam Qadir, her army consisted of "four *paltans* of sepoys trained for battle with 85 guns." Francklin, in his *Memoirs of George Thomas* (p. 32), in describing the events of 1794 says that at the time, the Begam's force was composed of "four battalions of infantry, 20 pieces of artillery and about 400 cavalry commanded by officers of tried and acknowledged abilities." Elsewhere Francklin records the strength of her forces, "based on a statement made by Mr. Thomas in 1802" (p. 267*n*), as follows:—5 battalions of about 600 men—3,000; pieces of artillery 24; and cavalry 150. Later on (in 1797-98)* their number was augmented still further. Major Lewis Ferdinand Smith, an officer attached to the army of Daulat Rao Sindhia, writes:—"Her army, in September 1803, consisted of 6 battalions or 4,000

* With his letter, dated Cawnpur 5 October 1798, (*Secret Cons.* 23-11-1798, Nos. 1, 2, & 7) J. Collins, Resident with Sindhia enclosed an account of the Begam's military force. But this document can be found neither in the Imperial Record Office, Calcutta, nor in the India Office, London.

fighting men, 40 pieces of cannon, and 200 cavalry."*

Immediately after the Begam's death Mr. R. N. C. Hamilton, the Magistrate and Collector of Meerut, prepared a detailed statement† showing the actual strength of her forces, ascertained on enquiries made by him. This statement gives the number of the different sections of her army as follows :—

Native Infantry			
1st Battalion	...	Total	507
2nd ,,	...	...	504
3rd ,,	...	...	504
4th ,,	...	...	488
5th ,,	...	...	481
6th ,,	...	...	462
			2,946
Men belonging to the Body-guard		...	266
Men belonging to Irregular Cavalry		...	245
Artillery Establishment	...	...	1,007
			4,464

* *A Sketch of the rise, progress and termination, of the Regular Corps, formed and commanded by Europeans, in the service of the Native princes of India*, etc. (1805), p. 5.

† Letter dated 28-1-1836 from R. N. C. Hamilton, Magistrate & Collector, Meerut, to J. R. Hutchinson, Commissioner 1st Dvn., Meerut.—*Pol. Con.* 22 Feby. 1836, No. 26.

After her treaty with the British, half of her troops, *viz.*, 3 battalions of native infantry and a small party of artillery, was set apart for the needs of the British and was placed under their orders. The respective places where these battalions were stationed and their number* are given below :—

2nd Battalion ...	...	516
At Rania	388	
At Bhawani	128	
3rd Battalion ...	...	515
At Meerut	259	
At Muzaffarnagar	194	
At Saharanpur	62	
5th Battalion ...	...	515
At Karnal	250	
At Gurgaon (Jharsa)	265	

From investigations conducted amongst the Begam's *daftars* in September 1805 by Mr. G. D. Guthrie, the Collector of Saharanpur, we find that the pay roll of one battalion in September

* Letter dated 17-4-1834 from W. Fraser, Agent to Govr.-Genl. to W. H. Macnaghten, Secy. to Govt., Fort Wm. —*Pol. Con.* 15-5-1834, Nos. 46-47.

1803 amounted to Rs. 6,595 plus Rs. 4,246 while serving in the Deccan. The pay of the officer in command of a brigade consisting of 3 or more battalions and his staff amounted to Rs. 541, plus Rs. 401 while in the Deccan. The pay of the Detachment staff, *i.e.*, the General Officer Commanding and his staff amounted to Rs. 865 without any extra allowance for Deccan service.*

After Sardhana had passed under British protection the constitution of the Begam's army was modified, resulting in a considerable curtailment of the expenses. The monthly costs of the Begam's troops on duty in the British provinces were Rs. 11,763 collectively for the 3 battalions, and Rs. 170-3-8 for the artillery detail at Hansi, 89 miles north-west of Delhi.†

The Begam's soldiers were well trained and warlike, and cosequently the higher British authorities wished to retain in their own service after her death

* For full details as to the strength of a battalion, see *Sect.* Con. 21-11-1805, No. 52A.

† Para 6 to letter dated 16-3-1836 from J. R. Hutchinson, Commissioner, 1st Meerut Dvn., to R. H. Scott, Offg. Secy. Pol. Dept., Allahabad.—*Pol. Con.* 23 May 1836, No. 67.

the portion of her troops stationed at Sardhana, besides those doing duty in the British provinces. But a month after her demise, the Magistrate of Meerut, before he could receive orders to this effect, paid up their dues and disbanded them. Several of them sought a new master in Ranjit Singh of Lahor.

Personal Landed Property

The Begam possessed many costly palaces and beautifully laid out gardens (*Refutation*, pp. 169-71, 374) at different places, which she visited in turn according to her fancy.

Her mansion at Delhi, known as *Churi wallon-ke Haveli*, stood within a very extensive garden. "Its parterres were thickly planted with the choicest fruits and flowers, and it was traversed by avenues of superb cypresses." This *haveli* still exists at Delhi. It is situated 150 yards to the north of the Chandni Chawk tram-line and stands facing the premises of the Alliance Bank of Simla built recently. Not far from it on the south lies the famous Jama Masjid. For several years past the offices of the Delhi

BEGAM'S DELHI PALACE

ST. JOHN'S SCHOOL—MEERUT

and London Bank occupied this mansion, but in 1922 it was purchased from the bank by a rich citizen of the locality.

It is stated by Major Archer that the Begam "possessed a garden near Bharatpur, and a good house within that fort" (i. 143). From a copy of the *sanad*,* now in the Imperial Record Office, Calcutta, we learn that 1,600 *bighas* of garden land at Deeg, near Bharatpur, belonging to her step-son, Zafar-yab Khan, were confirmed to him. This property passed into her hands after his death. In the above extract Major Archer must have referred to this land. "At Agra she had three gardens, and a market in the same district" (*Refutation*, pp. 171, 268).

In Meerut she had a large house with an extensive garden where she most often lived before her Sardhana palace was built (in 1834). This Meerut house, known as *Begam Kothi*, is now the property of a Muhammadan zamindar, and lies on the south of Meerut College.

---

* *Pol. Con.* 29 October 1832, No. 72. Afrasiab Khan, the adopted son of Mirza Najaf Khan, when became supreme, granted this *sanad* on 25 Rabi-us-sani [1195 H.] in the 23rd year of Shah Alam II's reign [20 April, 1781].

At Khirwa, five miles from Sardhana, she had another fine house which she was in the habit of visiting for a change of air. It was being built in February 1828, as mentioned by Major Archer, and "levelled to the ground in 1848" (*Refutation*, p. 334*n*). She had also a residential house at Jalalpur, the ruins of which were still in existence about 1874. (*N.-W. P. Gaz.* iii. 295, 430).

Some two years before her death in 1836, the Begam built a very beautiful two-storeyed palace in the Anglo-Indian style at Sardhana. The design and execution of the work was entrusted to Major Reghalini, an Italian officer in her service. It is known by the name of *Dilkusha Kothi* and is raised upon a basement 11 ft. in height. The palace and the grounds attached to it cover 75 acres, the whole being surrounded by a boundary wall.

Writing in 1880, Keene describes the other edifices of the Begam as follows: "On issuing from the park-gate, the visitor can turn to the right, where to the west of the palace he will find the *Camera*, or country-house, which was the Begam's last residence before the present palace was

Sardhana Palace

St. John's College—Sardhana

built. Proceeding in a southerly direction, he will pass an old garden-house where she lived when she first settled at Sardhana, protected by the guns of the adjoining fort, of which nothing is now visible, but the remains of some large earth-works. Going on in the same direction, he will find the cemetery, at present much neglected and choked with bushes and high grass.* The principal tomb is a large domed building to the memory of Julia Anne, daughter of Zafar-yab Khan ......and mother of Mr. Dyce Sombre. In the very centre of the enclosure a platform with a screen marks the resting place of poor Levassoult."

From the cemetery a walk through the town conducts the visitor to St. John's School—"sometimes, but incorrectly called a cathedral—a house once inhabited by the Begam, and now appropriated to purposes of education. . . . Under instructions in the will Mr. Dyce Sombre had made a deed of trust for the foundation of

* "Perhaps few know that it has been declared a protected monument and is now [1921] under Government which has begun the necessary repair and restorations" (*Sardhana & Its Begum*, editor's note, p. 19).

a seminary for the training of priests. This scheme has broken down, and the institution is now a mere school for native Christians* . . . A similar establishment for girls is carried on by the sisters residing in the convent" attached to the Cathedral Church of St. Mary which faces St. John's School.

The church is dedicated to the Blessed Virgin Mary. The Begam made some precious gifts of enduring interest to it.† Among the most noticeable objects in it are the high altar of white Jaipur marble inlaid with precious stones, and the monument in memory of the Begam.

"In the back of the northern transept stands a white marble group by Tadolini, of Rome,‡ erected by Mr. Dyce Sombre to

* But it is more of an orphanage than a college or anything else. "The school-house was presented to the trust by Baron Solaroli."—Col. T. B. Butt; see also *Sardhana*, editor's note, p. 15.

† For a list of these gifts, see Dyer's article in the *Calcutta Review*, April 1894, p. 316.

‡ Dyce Sombre's "agreement with the sculptor, Tadolini, was, that he was to receive one hundred thousand francs, [about Rs. 40,000] for the work (£ 4,000) when completed" (*Refutation* p. 276).

ST. MARY'S CATHEDRAL CHURCH—SARDHANA

the memory of his benefactress. It is pyramidal in character, and, allowing for the difficulties of the subject, is a very fine work. At the base sit figures, allegorizing the virtues of the deceased; and on the plinth are panels showing in high relief the state of Her Highness in *darbar*, in church, and at the head of her troops. At the four corners stand figures representing a priest [Bishop Julius Cæsar], a Persian writer [Diwan Rai Singh], Dyce Sombre [in the attitude of grief] in a general's uniform, and a native officer of cavalry [Inayetullah]. The whole is surmounted by a statue of Her Highness, in the act of administering justice." She, attired in Indian costume, is seated aloft on a chair of state, holding in her right hand a folded scroll, the Emperor's *farman*, conferring on her the *jagir* of Sardhana.

"Panels on the upper sides express in Latin and English, the inability of the

---

It is stated on page 48 of *Sardhana* and, following it by several other writers, that the monument was erected in 1842. But from a letter (*Refutation*, p. 279) dated 2nd October 1847 addressed to Dyce Sombre by his wife, we gather that the monument was not despatched to India till then, nor was it sent out prior to 6th December 1848 as is evidenced from the contents of a memorial of Dyce Sombre bearing the latter date. (*Ibid.* pp. 309, 333*n*).

founder to set forth duly the virtues and talents of the departed":

> Sacred to the memory of Her Highness Joanna Zeb-un-nisa, the Begam Sombre, styled the distinguished of nobles and beloved daughter of the State, who quitted a transitory Court for an eternal world, revered and lamented by thousands of her devoted subjects, at her palace of Sirdhanah, on the 27th of January, 1836, aged ninety years. Her remains are deposited underneath, in this Cathedral built by herself. To her powerful mind, her remarkable talent, and the wisdom, justice and moderation with which she governed for a period exceeding half a century, he to whom she was more than a mother is not the person to award the praise, but in grateful respect to her beloved memory is this monument erected by him who humbly trusts she will receive a crown of glory that fadeth not away.
>
> DAVID OCHTERLONY DYCE SOMBRE.

"At the foot rest his own poor bones, covered by a slab, giving the dates of his birth (1808)—marriage (1840)—and death 1851). Looking at these monuments, one can hardly fail to be forcibly impressed by a sense of the extraordinary vicissitudes which human life sometimes presents."*

---

* *Calcutta Rev.* 1880, pp. 461-62; *Sardhana*, pp. 10-11.

BEGAM'S STATUE—SARDHANA

CHAPTER IX

ADMINISTRATION AND POLICY

Instances are not rare in the history of India of persons rising from the humblest rank to the dizzy height of power, but it is doubtful whether many parallels can be found to the career of Begam Samru. For a poor homeless girl to rise to the rank of an independent ruler, and, what was more difficult, to maintain her position amidst political storms and convulsions that shattered old and powerful thrones, called for uncommon ability even in a man. All the more remarkable then it was for one belonging to the weaker sex to remove the innumerable difficulties that lay across her path and, while maintaining peace and prosperity in her domain, to take an active part in the political struggle of the country at large. As Capt. Francklin justly observes :

> "Endowed by nature with masculine intrepidity, assisted by a judgment and foresight clear and comprehensive, Begam Samru, during the various revolutions was enabled to

> preserve her country unmolested and her authority unimpaired" (*Shah-Aulum*, p. 147).

In her relations with other States she was guided by the desire to maintain her possessions unmolested, and hence she refrained from hostilities as far as possible. She was shrewd enough to realize that a mere friendly attitude, without an army at her back, would not be of much use at a time when several Powers were contending for supremacy in India. She therefore set herself to remodel and increase her army, whose reputation soon spread far and wide, and the Princess of Sardhana was respected and her friendship eagerly sought for by all. At one time she was the most powerful ally of the Emperor of Delhi and took a leading part in Delhi politics. The Emperor Shah Alam II, living in the midst of the treachery and machinations of enemies, and wearied with incessant political troubles and anxieties, could breathe freely and consider himself safe only when he chanced to have this noble lady by his side. It was no other than Begam Samru for whose help the second highest personage in the realm, Prince Jawan Bakht Jahandar Shah, had to apply when he resolved to have his father (the Emperor of Delhi) liberated from the clutches of the Marathas (*Ibratnama*, iii. 62-63). When there was an apprehension of Khande Rao Hari creating disturbances at Delhi, Prince Mirza Akbar had to solicit the Begam's co-operation.* Likewise, Ambaji Dhara Rao, the Maratha general, pursued the wise policy of conciliating the Begam along with other Maratha tributaries in order to resist the ambitious and dangerous designs of Zaman Shah, the grandson of Ahmad Shah Durraṇi.†

Perhaps at no time in her life was she called upon to display so much diplomacy as when dealing with the British Government during the Governor-Generalship of Wellesley. It 1804 she found herself in a very unenviable position, being faced with the prospect of having to give up her jagir in the Doab. There was very little

* *Dilli-yethil Marathanchin Rajkaranen*, ii. p. 100, dated 30-3-1794.

† Letter from J. Collins, Resident with Daulat Rao Sindhia, dated Fatehgarh, 9th December 1798. *Secret Consultation* 4-1-1799, No. 14.

chance of the promise of another territory in exchange materializing in the near future. As a result she grew suspicious of the intentions of the British. In order to force their hands she secretly stirred up disturbances in the Doab and the surrounding districts, but so cleverly did she manage it that even Lord Wellesley, astute politician though he was, was helpless in this matter, although he was fully aware of the facts. She completely hoodwinked Lord Lake, to whose discretion was left the management of the affairs in the Doab. Her rescue of Mr. Guthrie disarmed Lake's suspicions to such an extent that he issued orders that on no account should she be attacked, as he was convinced that the Begam's friendship and co-operation were absolutely necessary in order to preserve the tranquillity of the Doab.

Except for this passing estrangement from the British, the Begam's relations with them were friendly and her services were warmly appreciated by them. In a letter, dated 9th July 1807, to the Secretary to Government (Pol. Dept.), Mr. Archibald Seton, the Resident at Delhi, says:

> "It is impossible for me, as a Briton, to withhold the tribute of gratitude so justly due to her successful endeavours to effect the delivery of General (then Col.) Stuart from the Sikhs, and at a later period, to her seasonable exertions in favour of Mr. Guthrie [Collector of Saharanpur] when in danger of falling into the hands of that ferocious people" (*Refutation*, p. 404).

Speaking of her ability as a diplomat and administrator, Major Archer, Aide-de-camp to Lord Combermere, writes:

> "She has, through a long life, maintained her station and security among a host of contending powers, and may bear the honour of a similarity of character with our Elizabeth" (i. 142).

Within the *jagir* her power was absolute and the whole administration, whether civil or criminal, was vested in her.* She was a wise and benevolent ruler and turned her attention chiefly to the increase of the wealth and prosperity of her territory and the suppression of crime.

---

* "The old lady enjoys the right of judicature upon her own ground, but in criminal cases, she is obliged to inform the British Government of her intention before she can bring a man to capital punishment"—Bacon, ii. 53; see also *P. C. Judgments*, Badshapur Suit, p. 2.

Under her beneficent rule the tenantry lived in peace and plenty, and were happy and contented at the security of their life and property being assured. She was always keenly alive to their interests, and in times of drought and hardship assisted them with *taqavi** or agricultural loans and thus saved them from ruin and starvation. Major Archer, who visited Sardhana in 1828, writes (i. 142) thus about the prosperous state of her jagir:

> "She has turned her attention to the agricultural improvement of her country, though she knows she is planting that which others will reap. Her fields look greener and more flourishing and the population of her villages appear happier and more prosperous than those of the Company's provinces. Her care is unremitting and her protection sure."

It is no wonder then that those who had occasion to travel in the Begam's jagir were favourably impressed with its flourishing appearance and the prosperity of her subjects, which contrasted sharply with the desolation and distress prevailing

* "In realizing the revenue the *taqavi* advances were first recovered with interest at 25 per cent per annum" (*N.-W.P. Gaz.* iii. 432).

in the surrounding lands. The visitors to Sardhana spoke in warm appreciation of her good and wise government, the prosperous condition of her estate, and the respect which her people paid to her:*

> "An unremitting attention to the cultivation of the lands, a mild and upright administration, and care for the welfare of the inhabitants, has enabled this small tract to vie with the most cultivated parts of Hindustan, and to yield a revenue of ten lakhs of Rupees per annum" (Francklin's *Shah-Aulum,* p. 147).

But, on the other hand, Mr. T. C. Plowden in his *Settlement Report* of 1840, as quoted by Atkinson in *N.-W. P. Gazetteer*, iii., says:

> "She appropriated the whole produce of their [her tenants'] labour, with the exception of what sufficed to keep body and soul together . . . . . and by nicely keeping the balance, and always limiting her demand to the exact point of endurance, and with equally due regard to favourable or unfavourable seasons, . . . a fictitious state of prosperity was induced and maintained, which though it might, and I believe did, deceive the Begam's neighbours into an impression that her country was highly prosperous, could not delude the population into content and

* *Asiatic Journal,* vol. xv. Septr.-Decr. 1834, p. 147.

happiness. Above the surface and to the eye all was smiling and prosperous, but within was rottenness and misery."*

Atkinson further says:

"As long as the Begam retained possession of her energy and strength, this system flourished. But when her heir attempted to meddle in the administration, during the last few years of her life, the fictitious nature of the prosperity of her estates became apparent."

Shortly after the death of the Begam an anonymous article appeared in the *Meerut Universal Magazine*,† in which the writer remarked that owing to merciless rack-renting her tenantry constantly fled in despair to the British possessions for protection, and that the presence of armed soldiers in the fields was sometimes

---

* See Appendix *D*.

† "Some Remarks on the Principality of Sirdhanah"—*M. U. Mag.* (iv. 1837), pp. 274-79. This is most probably the article which Keene (*Cal. Review*, 1880, p. 463) describes as contributed by a competent observer (H. M. Elliot) to the *M. U. Mag.*, shortly *before* the Begam's death in 1836, as no trace of any article from the pen of Mr. Elliot can be found in any issue of the above magazine prior to the Begam's death.

I take this opportunity of expressing my gratefulness to Major B. D. Basu of Allahabad for granting me the loan of the *M. U. Mag.* for 1837.

necessary to keep the ploughmen at their work. He even went so far as to say that "not a trace of a single improvement of any description, throughout her territory, for the amelioration of her subjects and country could be found" (p. 276).

Both Plowden and Elliot were English Government officials, and it is therefore not unlikely that their criticism of the Begam's administration was influenced by their admiration for the British system which was then replacing it. It seems to have been the case that Dyce Sombre, who had charge of the Begam's estate during the last few years of her life, increased the revenue to some extent, and this might have tended to displease some of her subjects. Plowden made the revenue settlement of the estate after the Begam's death, and his remarks might apply to the state of affairs prevailing at that time ; but in view of the observations of Archer, Francklin, and other European contemporaries of rank and position, we are not inclined to agree with Plowden's inference of the condition of the State as well as of the subjects under the Begam's personal administration.

All who came in contact with this noble lady have testified with one voice that her mind was large and liberal to a degree and that she was kind and considerate at heart. The universal cry of sorrow that arose at her death was a proof of the love and regard which her subjects bore towards her, and which she fully reciprocated.

It is a pity that Bishop Heber, Victor Jacquemont, and a few other writers, who came to Sardhana as casual visitors, too readily accepted false and flimsy rumours, and did not feel the least hesitation in charging the Begam with the blackest cruelty and barbarism. Their portraiture was based on the following incident, narrated by Sleeman:

> "While she was encamped [in 1782, see *N.-W.P. Gaz.* ii. 91] with the army of the prime-minister of the time at Mathura, news was one day brought to her that two slave-girls had set fire to her houses at Agra, in order that they might make off with their paramours, two soldiers of the guard she had left in charge. These houses had thatched roofs, and contained all her valuables, and the widows, wives, and children of her principal officers. The fire had been put out

> with much difficulty and great loss of property ; and the two slave-girls were soon after discovered in the bazar at Agra, and brought out to the Begam's camp. She had the affair investigated in the usual summary form ; and their guilt being proved to the satisfaction of all present, she had them flogged till they were senseless, and then thrown into a pit dug in front of her tent for the purpose, and buried alive. I had heard the story related in different ways, and I now took pains to ascertain the truth ; and this short narrative may, I believe, be relied upon" (Sleeman, ii. 274).

We have no means now of testing the truth of the tale. But at the worst it amounts to this that under exceptional circumstances the Begam had recourse to a severe punishment in order to keep some turbulent spirits in check. According to the standard of modern civilization, burying a person alive would certainly be a monstrous crime smacking of mediæval barbarism ; we shudder at the bare thought of it. But at the time when this cruel punishment was prescribed, it was not considered so very heinous, as history abounds in instances of the actual infliction of punishments more terrible than this. It is, therefore, not reasonable to pronounce a sweeping condemnation upon the character of the Begam, without considering the prevailing practices of the time and the circumstances under which the sentence was passed. Penal laws change with changing circumstances and manners.

By the infliction of capital punishment on the slave-girls she gave vicious-minded people to understand that she would not flinch from suppressing crime. Sir W. H. Sleeman remarks:

> "I am satisfied that the Begam believed them guilty, and that the punishment, horrible as it was, was merited. It certainly had the desired effect. My object has been to ascertain the truth in this case, and to state it, and not to eulogize or defend the old Begam" (ii. 275-76).

The greatness of a person is measured more by the warmth of his heart than by the capacity of his brains, and, judged by this criterion, our princess was pre-eminently a noble being whose heart would melt at the sight of another's miseries. Her religious devotion and charitable disposition lent a charm to her exemplary character, and endeared and exalted her name. She earned the blessings of the poor and the destitute by helping them unreservedly and the intensity of her solicitude for the welfare of the people can be best measured by the total extent of her charitable gifts, amounting to the princely sum of about eight lakhs of Rupees, which was utilized for building places of worship and works conducive to the general weal. Even leaving out of consideration her other virtues, her memory will ever be cherished with love by the people of India for the uncommon benevolence of her heart and the splendour of her charity. Governor-General Lord William Bentinck, an excellent judge of character, on the eve of his departure from India, addressed her the following letter expressing his esteem for her character :

To

HER HIGHNESS THE BEGAM SOMBRE.

My esteemed friend,

I cannot leave India without expressing the sincere esteem I entertain for your Highness's character. The benevolence of disposition and extensive charity which have endeared you to thousands, have excited in my mind sentiments of the warmest admiration ; and I trust that you may yet be preserved for many years the solace of the orphan and widow, and the sure resource of your numerous dependents. To-morrow morning I embark for England, and my prayers and best wishes attend you, and all others who like you exert themselves for the benefit of the people of India.

I remain,
With much consideration,
Your sincere friend,
W. C. BENTINCK.

Calcutta,
March, 17th 1835.

APPENDIX *D*

ADVERSE CRITICISM OF HER ADMINISTRATION.*

After the Begam's death, the revenue settlement of her estate was made by Mr. T. C. Plowden. Mr. E. T. Atkinson, who has largely drawn upon Mr. Plowden's *Settlement Report* of 1840, observes in his *N.-W. P. Gazetter*:

"The cultivators were only left sufficient to keep body and soul together. Mr. Plowden writes:—'The rule seems to have been fully recognized and acted up to by the Begam which declared that according to Muhammadan law "there shall be left for every man who cultivates his lands as much as he requires for his own support, till the next crop be reaped, and that of his family and for seed. This much shall be left to him; what remains is land-tax and shall go to the public treasury." For considering her territory as a private estate and her subjects as serfs, she appropriated the whole produce of their labour, with the exception of what sufficed to keep body and soul together. It was by these means, and by nicely keeping the balance, and always limiting her demand to the exact point of endurance, and with equally due regard to favourable or unfavourable seasons, that a fictitious state of prosperity was induced and

* *N.-W.P. Gaz.* iii. 283-84, 431-33; *M. U. Magazine*, (Agra, 1837). iv. 274-79.

maintained, which though it might, and I believe did, deceive the Begam's neighbours into an impression that her country was highly prosperous, could not delude the population into content and happiness. Above the surface and to the eye all was smiling and prosperous, but within was rottenness and misery. Under these circumstances the smallness of the above arrear is no proof of the fairness of the revenue. It rather shows that the collections were as much as the Begam's ingenuity could extract, and this balance being unrealizable, the demand was by so much at least too high.'

"As long as the Begam retained possession of her energy and strength, this system, the product of her own tact and shrewdness, flourished. But when her heir attempted to meddle in the administration, during the last few years of her life, the fictitious nature of the prosperity of her estates became apparent. He abandoned the old system and its advances and made a settlement for three years. Adopting the old demand *plus* cesses, he allowed only a set-off of five per cent and attempted to collcet the rest as regular revenue. The net revenue of this settlement for 1243 *fasli* [1835-36] was Rs. 6,91,388, exclusive of 35 villages held *kham*. This resulted in an increase of a lakh of Rupees in the demand, while no assistance was rendered in bad seasons or when untoward circumstances affected the cultivator. The result may be easily imagined ; in the first year of the lease 92 villages fell under direct management, in the second six, and in the third 28 more villages, amounting to one-third of the whole estate. Ruin was impending, when the Begam's death, in January 1836, and the consequent lapse of the estate to the British, induced the cultivators to return to their homes" (*Gaz.* iii. 433).

CHAPTER X

GLIMPSES OF THE COURT OF SARDHANA

Very little information about the private life of the famous Sardhana Princess can be gleaned from the contemporary writers. She could boast of no illustrious heritage, and, while she was the wife of General Sombre, she had no independent position at the Mughal *darbar*. Even at the height of her power when the Princess of Sardhana was known to all, she preferred to live in her principality and so in the narratives of the Court of Delhi we find no description of her person or following, although her name is occasionally mentioned. Most of our information about her personality is derived from the *Military Memoirs of George Thomas*, who was her general for some time, and from occasional records left by the visitors to her Court after she had come under the protection of the British.

In youth she must have been a strikingly handsome woman. Geo. Thomas describes her personal appearance in 1796 as follows:

> "Begam Samru is about forty-five years of age, small in stature, but inclined to be plump. Her complexion is very fair, her eyes black, large and animated. Her dress perfectly Hindustani and of the most costly materials. She speaks the Persian and Hindustani languages with fluency, and in her conversation is engaging, sensible and spirited" (*Thomas*, p. 59*n*).

A decade later, a lady observer, Mrs. A. Deane, visited Sardhana and has left for us this pen-portrait of the Begam:

> "Her features are still handsome, although she is now advanced in years. She is a small woman, delicately formed, with beautiful hazel eyes; a nose somewhat inclined to the aquiline, a complexion very little darker than an Italian, with the finest turned hand and arm I ever beheld. Zophany, the painter, when he saw her, pronounced it a perfect model. She is universally attentive and polite. A graceful dignity accompanies her most trivial actions; she *can be* even fascinating, when she has any point to carry" (p. 150).

Although she used to march in person with her battalions in most of their campaigns, in her earlier days she also strictly maintained Indian etiquette, and the Memoirs of Geo. Thomas give us an insight into her life at Sardhana:

> "It has been the constant and invariable usage of this lady, to exact from her subjects and servants the most rigid attention to the customs of Hindustan. She is never seen out of doors, or in her public darbar unveiled. Her officers and others, who have business with her, present themselves opposite the place where she sits; the front of her apartments is furnished with *chiques* or Indian screens, these being let down from the roof; in this manner she gives audience, and transacts business of all kinds. She frequently admits to her table the higher ranks of her European officers, but never admits the natives to come within the inclosure. On dinner being announced, twenty or thirty of her female attendants, most of them Christians, repairing to the outer door, there receive the dishes and place them upon table, they wait on the company during the repast, which is always plentiful and well served" (*Thomas*, pp. 58-59).

But later on, she changed her manner of living, as is thus described by Mrs. Deane:

"She adheres to the Musalman mode of living, as far as respects food, and but no further. She has not the slightest fancy for the seclusion they impose; on the contrary, frequently entertaining large parties in a sumptuous manner, both at her palace in Delhi and at Sardhana. During Lord Lake's sojourn at Delhi, he was her frequent guest. They used frequently to sit down between twenty and thirty persons to dinner; and when the ladies of the party retired, she would remain smoking her hookah, for she made it a point never to leave her 'pipe half smoked'" (p. 149).

Sleeman says the same thing:

"She by degrees adopted the European modes of social intercourse, appearing in public on an elephant, in a carriage, and occasionally on horseback with her hat and veil, and dining at table with gentlemen. She often entertained Governors-General and Commanders-in-chief, with all their retinues, and sat with them and their staff at table, and for some years past kept an open house for the society of Meerut; but in no situation did she lose sight of her dignity" (*Rambles*, ii. 288).

"At the dinner the Begam seemed in excellent humour, and bandied jokes and compliments . . . through the medium of an interpreter" (Mundy, i. 376).

As a matter of fact in her conversation she always managed to interest the audience.

As for the Begam's costume, she used to have her little person enveloped in a yellow Cashmere shawl of exquisite texture; under this shawl a handsome green silk cloak of European fashion, but embroidered, was generally worn. Mrs. Deane noted, about 1809, that "contrary to the practice of women in this country, the Begam Samru always wears a turban, generally damson colour, which becomes her very much, and is put on with great taste" (p. 159). Her slippers were as bright and as small as those of Cinderella. Upon most occasions she was decorated with a prodigious quantity of jewels.

Her stud of horses was one of the finest in Hindustan. As Mrs. Deane writes:

> "We saw a number of fine horses in her stables, and an English coach that had been lately built for her in Calcutta, which was to be drawn by four of them, with two postilions. I had afterwards the pleasure of accompanying her in it. The carriage was painted a bright yellow, with silver mouldings, lined with violet-coloured satin, embroidered all over with silver stars. The window frames

of solid silver ; the lace and hangings silver ribbon, wove in a pattern, and very substantial, with silver bullion tassels. The wheels were dark blue, to match the lining. The postilions wore scarlet jackets and caps, almost covered with silver lace" (pp. 178-9).

She had a fine band of European musicians, under a M. Antoine. After her death, he sought service with Ranjit Singh, who was anxious to secure good European bandsmen for teaching their art to his own people.*

The Begam usually gave a grand féte during Christmas, which lasted for three days, and to which all the European society of Meerut, Delhi, and the surrounding stations was invited.

"Tents are prepared in the palace-garden for the accommodation of visitors, and every luxury which a profuse outlay can secure is provided for the company ; the tables are sumptuously spread, the viands and the wines are alike excellent. Upon these grand occasions, the Begam usually honours the guests by presiding at the table ; but she does not partake of any food in their presence. Not only

---

* Ranjit Singh's letter, dated 6th March 1836, to Lala Kishan Chand, his agent at Ludhiana, seeking the permission of the English agent there to entertain these men. (*Pol. Con.* 2 May 1836, No. 57).

are the numerous visitors entertained in this magnificent style, but the whole host of their followers and train are also feasted and fêted, in a manner equally sumptuous in proportion to their condition" (Bacon, ii. 51).

Mrs. Deane has left a graphic account of the Court festivities at Sardhana:

"At the Begam Samru's palace we found thirty persons of rank assembled, and a splendid banquet in the European style. This ended, she arose and threw over the shoulders of each of the ladies a wreath of flowers formed of a tuberose plant, united by narrow gold ribbon. No sooner was she re-seated, than strains of soft music were heard, and two folding doors of the saloon flew open as if by enchantment, discovering a number of young girls in the attitude of dancing a ballet, or, as it is here termed, a *notch*. It appeared to me, however, little more than a display of attitudes; indeed their feet and ancles were so shackled by a large gold ring, of more than an inch in thickness, and bells strung round another, that springing off the ground must have been impracticable; in fact, their dancing consisted in jingling these bells in unison with the notes of the musical instruments, which were played by men educated for that purpose. To this music they give effect by appropriate motions of hands, arms, and person, not forgetting

> that more expressive vehicle of the sentiments, *the eyes.* Their movements were by no means devoid of grace, particularly when accompanied by the voice" (p. 169).

Bacon adds to this picture:

> "She was particularly affable to European ladies, and seldom permitted them to quit her presence without bestowing upon them some token of her generosity, according to the native custom, either a Cashmere shawl, or a piece of silk, or a jewel, to the value of 20 or 30 guineas" (*ibid.* ii. 46).

He remarks with quite a natural surprise:

> "When we recollect who the Begam originally was, the diabolical character of her husband, ...it is strange thus to find an enlightened British community, the victors of the soil, doing homage and seeking favour at her footstool, or even condescending to partake of her hospitality" (ii. 52).

Although she lavishly feasted and féted the visitors to her Court, she herself lived a very plain life and spent most of her time in looking after the State affairs. She was a resolute and untiring worker, and managed all her affairs in person. She did her duty with the utmost deliberation, carefully weighing the pros and cons of every action, and being seldom carried away by any impulse of the moment. She had confidence in herself and a great regard for justice; she usually displayed uncommon sagacity and masculine firmness, and her presence of mind was also remarkable. On 29th October, 1803, Lord Lake wrote to the Begam to come alone to his camp on some urgent matter which required her presence. The Begam getting into her palanquin hastened to the British camp, which was then situated at Pahesar, 13 miles west of Bharatpur.

> "Upon this occasion an incident occurred of a curious and characteristic description. She arrived at head-quarters, it appears, just after dinner, and being carried in her palanquin at once to the reception tent, his lordship came out to meet and receive her. As the adhesion of every petty chieftain was, in those days, of consequence, Lord Lake was not a little pleased at the early demonstration of the Begam's loyalty; and being a little elevated by the wine which had just been drunk, he forgot the novel circumstance of its being a native female he was about to receive, instead of some well-bearded chief, so he gallantly advanced, and, to the utter dismay of her attendants, took her in his arms and kissed her. The

mistake might have been awkward, but the lady's presence of mind put all right. Receiving courteously the proffered attention, she turned calmly round to her astonished attendants—'It is,' said she, 'the salute of a *padre* (or priest) to his daughter.' The Begam professes Christianity, and thus the explanation was perfectly in character, though more experienced spectators might have smiled at the appearance of the jolly red-coated clergyman, exhibited in the person of his lordship" (Skinner, i. 293-94; Pearse's *Memoir of Lake*, pp. 252-53).

The same testimony is borne to her masculine capacity by a cultivated observer of her own sex:

"This woman has an uncommon share of natural abilities, with a strength of mind rarely met with, particularly in a female. The natives say that she was *born* a politician, has *allies* everywhere, and *friends* nowhere" (Mrs. Deane's *Tour*, p. 149).

Sleeman was informed by men capable of judging character, who had known her for more than fifty years, that "though a woman and of small stature, her *ruh* (dignity, or power of commanding personal respect) was greater than that of almost any person they had ever seen" (*Rambles*, ii. 288). It so happened that "on her excursions to Delhi, during the latter part of her life, she did not pay the usual tribute of homage to the Resident, of a visit, which, as the representative of the British Government he had a right to expect from all persons of inferior rank" (*As. Journal*, 1834, Sep.-Dec., p. 148; Bacon, ii. 53-54). The vanity of the official was wounded, and he went to the length of reporting the matter to the authorities. In the same year a misunderstanding also arose between the Begam and the Emperor Akbar Shah [*acc.* 1806], the successor of Shah Alam II, on a point of etiquette. "Akbar Shah, being pre-eminent by birth, the pure stock of the ancient Mughal dynasty, and being upon his own ground in the city of Delhi, insisted upon receiving homage from all of an inferior degree who met him," and the proud Begam, although not one of his subjects, was compelled "to have her elephant kneel down to the Emperor when passing him. This her vanity would not brook, and having been more than once compelled against her will thus to do reverence to a higher prince, she had for several years refrained from visiting Delhi" (Bacon, ii. 53-54)—once her favourite residence—rather than put her self-respect in danger of further affront.

Her wonderful mental powers remained unimpaired to the end of her long and eventful life. As late as December 1830, the French traveller Victor Jacquemont noted of her, "She is, in fine, a sort of walking mummy, who still looks after all her affairs herself, listens to two or three secretaries at once, and at the same time dictates to as many others" (*Letters*, ii. 247).

The curtain has long been rung down and the actress has passed away from the scene of her activities into the abode of bliss. But the stage is still in evidence; Sardhana is yet to be seen with the Begam's palace and the splendid shrine erected by her as a place of worship. But she who at one time reigned supreme there—the friend of the poor and their never-failing fountain of hope and delight—is no more; her dust has returned to dust, but her name endures for ever in her noble deeds.

CHAPTER XI

THE HISTORY OF THE BEGAM'S FORTUNE

Millions of Jules Verne's young readers in many lands have read with delight his fascinating novel, *The Begum's Fortune*, with its deep undercurrent of contrast between French humanity and German ruthlessness, written in the bitterness of the defeat at Sedan and Metz and the loss of Alsace and Lorraine. But how many of them know that the starting-point of the story, namely the legacy of a vast fortune left by an Indian princess to two Europeans, was suggested to him by a case which created some stir in England and France in this author's boyhood and whose history was published in Paris in 1849? The history of the heritage of Begam Samru, from its inception to its sale under the auctioneer's hammer in 1896, reads like a romance.

General Sombre was twice married and he left a son, by his first Muhammadan wife, named Zafar-yab Khan. This son of Sombre was baptized and married to

Juliana,* the daughter of Capt. Lefevre, and died leaving an only daughter (*b.* 19 Nov. 1789) named Julia Anne, who was given in marriage to Col. G. A. Dyce, a Scotchman in the Begam's service, on 8th October 1806. The Colonel had numerous issues, but with the exception of a son and two daughters all of them died in infancy. The son, born on 8th December 1808, was named David Ochterlony Dyce, and the daughters Anne Mary (*b.* 24 Feby. 1812) and Georgiana (*b.* 1815). On the death of the Colonel's wife at Delhi, on 13th June 1820, Begam Samru took charge of her children and brought them up as her own. The girls Anne and Georgiana, when grown to womanhood, were respectively given in marriage on 3rd August 1831, to two worthy Europeans in her service—Capt. Rose Troup, formerly of the Bengal Army, and Paul Solaroli, an Italian (afterwards Marquis of Briona), and both of them received handsome dowries from the Begam.

---

* Juliana was also known as Bahu Begam. She was buried in the Catholic cemetery at Sardhana, and from the inscription on her tomb we learn that she died, aged 45, on 18th October 1815. (*Sardhana*, pp. 20-21).

Col. G. A. Dyce, who had for some time the management of the Begam's affairs, both civil and military, was in the intimate confidence of his mistress, who at one time conceived the desire of appointing him her heir, but he "lost her favour long before her death by his violent temper and overbearing manners, and was obliged to resign the management" (Sleeman, ii. 286) in 1827. Bacon says (ii. 47), "he was ejected under pretext of covert communications with the British Government." His son David Ochterlony Dyce was installed in his post at the head of affairs. After this disagreeable incident the Colonel's conduct towards the Begam became hostile to a degree, nor was he well disposed even towards his son.

The Begam had no children of her own and seemed, therefore, to be designed by Providence, to play the róle of a mother to a motherless child. She loved David Ochterlony Dyce with her whole being and was more than a mother to him, taking particular care to have him educated. The Revd. Mr. Fisher, Chaplain to the E. I. Co. at Meerut, in the immediate neighbourhood of the Begam's residence, acted for a time as tutor to young David. Bacon, a contemporary European, writes:

> "Dyce was educated at the Delhi College, and is an excellent Persian and English scholar, and although very young, is said to be both active and politic in the discharge of his multifarious duties......He is a man of enormous bulk...and though his complexion is very dark, he has a very fine open countenance, expressive of mildness and intelligence. In disposition he is kind, and as generous as day light ; and he is a general favourite with all who know him" (ii. 48).

David's brilliant attainments and his charming disposition made him a special favourite with the Begam who gained some respite from toil in her old age by placing the management of her vast property in his hands. This good fortune of young Dyce kindled the fire of jealousy in the breast of many a man in the Begam's service.

Dyce Sombre came in for the bulk of the Begam's fortune.* Among other

* Besides the amount left to Dyce Sombre, the Begam bequeathed a further sum of 3,57,000 Sonat Rupees, thus divided :—(a) Rs. 70,000 to Col. Clemence Brown for his services as a joint executor. (b) Rs. 1,57,000 to a number

bequests, he received from her a sum of two *lakhs* of Rupees, but it was stipulated in the will that until he attained the age of 30, he would only enjoy the annual income of this amount which Col. Brown, a joint executor, was directed to invest. In a letter, dated 12th March 1836, (*Pol. Con.* 23-5-1836, No. 73) from the Magistrate of Meerut we observe that Her Highness left behind her nearly half a *krore* of Rupees (47,88,600 Sicca) in Government securities, which must have

---

of her most intimate friends, dependents and relatives; included among which were John Thomas, another of her adopted sons and the son of the celebrated adventurer George Thomas (Rs. 18,000), his wife Joanna (Rs. 7,000), and his mother Maria Thomas (Rs. 7,000); Anthony Reghalini, latterly a captain in her service (Rs. 9,000), Victoria his wife (Rs. 11,000), his five children (Rs. 5,000 a-piece); Abul Hasan Beg a commandant in her service (Rs. 2,000). (c) The interest of fifty and eighty thousand Sonat Rupees—to be held in trust—to Dyce Sombre's two sisters Anne Mary and Georgiana respectively. (d) To all and every one of her servants whether public or private who should happen to be in her service at the time of her death, one month's salary in addition to their arrears, if any. [Prior to his departure for England Dyce Sombre settled £ 20,000—Rupees two *lakhs*—on each of his two sisters.—*Refutation*, pp. 55, 322].

The Begam "previous to her demise directed that her medical attendant, Dr. Thomas Drever, should be paid in cash the sum of Rs. 20,000" (*Pol. Con.* 22-2-1836, No. 26; Bacon, ii. 59).

passed into the hands of Dyce Sombre. In addition to this, all her ornaments, jewels, household furniture, wearing apparel and even her elephants, horses and stock of every description came into his possession, along with the lands, houses, gardens &c. held by the Begam at Agra, Delhi, Bharatpur, Meerut, Sardhana, and other places. The only properties from which he was kept out were the pargana Badshapur-Jharsa on the west of the Jamuna and the *mauza* Bhogipura-Shahganj in *subah* Akbarabad (Agra). These, as well as the military stores,* were seized by the Company, when the jagir lapsed on the Begam's death. Dyce Sombre never submitted to this loss, though he instituted no suit for their possession. He objected, remonstrated, memorialized, represented himself as unjustly treated, and being foiled in his efforts to have his rights vindicated, he in despair at last "made

* Dyce Sombre "valued the military stores—such as arms, accoutrements for the soldiers, guns and other military appointments, magazine stores, powder, shot and shells—at Rs. 492,092" (*Refutation*. p. 396*n*), *i.e.*, close upon five *lakhs*, although he "did not ask for the value of the buildings, such as forts, offices etc" (*ibid*. p. 446*n*).

over his claims in a letter addressed to Her Majesty Queen Victoria" (*Refutation*, p. 346).*

---

* The representatives of Dyce Sombre, in a costly litigation which finally came before the Privy Council for decision, claimed to recover from the Government of India possession of the pargana Badshapur-Jharsa, a valuable estate, with mesne profits since August 1836. They did not claim merely a zamindari interest in the lands but wanted to hold them rent-free, *i.e.*, free from assessment to Government revenue, and the total value of the claim was assessed in round numbers at a sum little short of a quarter of a million sterling. The allegations of the appellants *inter alia* were that the pargana in dispute was an *altamgha*—a grant in perpetuity and as such could not be considered as forming part of the Begam's jagir. According to the treaty of 1805 between the Begam and the Company, "those places within the Doab" were liable to be résumed by the Company after her death, but Badshapur-Jharsa is situated beyond the Doab and the Company therefore had not the least justification to seize it. The respondents held that by virtue of the treaty of the 30th December 1803 the sovereignty over the Doab and the territories to the west of the Jamuna in which Badshapur is situated, passed from Daulat Rao Sindhia to the E. I. Co. and the Begam only continued to hold it during her lifetime along with her Doab jagir. But, in order to substantiate their claim, the appellants could not produce the original patent, granted by the Emperor of Delhi in favour of the Begam's step-son Zafar-yab Khan, in whose name the pargana had formerly stood, and what they did produce was a "copy" (*Refutation*, pp. 373-83) of a fabricated *sanad* bearing the seal of Mahadji Sindhia who had died in the beginning of the previous year. The Judicial Committee of the Privy Council after weighing the pros and the cons, gave its judgment in the case on 11th May 1872

At the age of thirty Dyce Sombre became the absolute master of a vast fortune. He was without any legal control on his actions, nor had he any honest adviser to guide him. He had a strong desire to visit the West and see for himself all the wonders of which he had heard so much. "Two of the Begam's old friends gave the young heir opposite advice the one to the other. Lord Combermere wrote warmly urging him to visit Europe; and Col. Skinner, C.B. addressed him an ode in Persian, strongly dissuading him from the step. The advice of the Colonel was better than that of the Field-marshal, in spite of which the latter prevailed" (*Cal. Rev.* 1880, p. 458). It is true that Dyce Sombre was born and brought up in India, but his father was Scotch and it was natural that he should long to see the home of his ancestors.

---

in favour of the respondents. It was however proved that the arms and military stores seized by the Company were actually purchased by the Begam at her own cost, and the heirs of Dyce Sombre should get the value of same with interest.

I would refer my readers to the *Privy Council Judgments* in which a complete history of the case will be found summed up.

With the object of visiting England he came to Calcutta in 1837, but his departure was postponed for a year as "his father Col. Dyce had instituted proceedings in the Supreme Court of Calcutta against him, as Executor of the will of the Begam, and claimed to receive from the estate of Her Highness the sum of fourteen lakhs" (*Pol. Con.*). We observe from Dyce Sombre's writings (*Reftn.*, 346) that Col. Dyce's claim was on account of "arrears of pay for nine years." The suit, however, was settled by compromise, and shortly afterwards Dyce Sombre sailed for England leaving his brother-in-law, Paul Solaroli, in charge of the management of his estates and properties. Thus, the father and son parted never to meet on earth again. Col. Dyce died in Calcutta in the month of April 1838 and was buried in Fort William.

Dyce Sombre reached England in June 1838 and in the following year he visited Rome, where he wished to commemorate the third Anniversary of the Begam's death (27 Jan. 1839), in a manner "proportioned both to her rank and to his affection. The magnificent Church of San

Carlo in Corso was selected for the purpose, and adorned with mournful splendour......High Mass was celebrated, accompanied by music of the most splendid character, and admirably conducted." And in the course of the morning, a Funeral Oration was delivered by the Very Revd. N. Wiseman, D. D., Rector of the English College, Rome. (*Sardhana*, pp. 48, 55-64).

Dyce Sombre, naturally enough, came in for a good deal of notice in England. In the beginning of August 1838 he became acquainted with Mary Anne Jervis, the only surviving daughter of Edward Jervis, second Viscount St. Vincent, and they were married two years afterwards (26 Sept. 1840), when the bride was aged about 28. In the following year Dyce Sombre was elected member of Parliament for the borough of Sudbury.

But this matrimonial connection, far from contributing in the least to his peace and felicity, became the cause of his unhappiness and ruin. After a short time there arose a considerable tension of feeling between the couple, so much so that Dyce Sombre plainly charged her with conduct unbecoming a true wife, and had occasion even to suspect her fidelity. Mrs. Dyce Sombre was tired of her husband's society. His acts seemed eccentric to her, and an attempt on her part to have him pronounced a lunatic, in which she was materially assisted by the two brothers-in-law of her husband—Capt. Rose Troup and Paul Solaroli, who bore him grudge,* was in the end successful.

Mrs. Dyce Sombre now began to show anxiety for the health of her husband and an officious doctor—as Dyce himself puts it—was called in. Then one fine morning Dyce Sombre rose to find himself a prisoner under the charge of three keepers at his doors. He was detained in captivity for more than 16 weeks before a Commission sat (31st July 1843) at his residence to enquire into the state of his mind. This Commission declared him to be of unsound mind and, as such, quite unfit to

---

* They frequently asserted to Mrs. Dyce Sombre that a pargana of great value [Badshapur] belonged in part to their wives, and that Dyce Sombre unlawfully kept from his sisters the evidence of their right contained in the original grant thereof or that he had destroyed it, in order to further his purpose of obtaining the whole for himself. (*Refutation*, p. 60).

be entrusted with the management of his own affairs.

But fortunately for him, Dyce escaped the effects of the lunacy decision. After the Commission had found him insane, his health began to fail and he was sent under a doctor to travel to Bristol and from thence to Liverpool. At the latter place he managed to elude his keepers in the morning of 21st September 1843, and arrived the following evening in Paris, without money and without any property except what he carried on his person. He had not a single *sou* given to him for several weeks when he was obliged to live on the advances of his friends. A Committee was soon formed to manage the affairs of the lunatic. What an irony of fate! He who was most tenderly brought up in the midst of affluence and princely comforts as the master of an enormous fortune, "yielding an income of £20,000 [two *lakhs* of Rupees] a year" (*Refutation*, pp. 53, 245) was at last compelled to live upon a poor pittance doled out to him by the Committee. And all the while the wife of Dyce Sombre was enjoying an allowance of £4,000 (Rs. 40,000) annually from his estates!

In order to prove his sanity before the world and to give the lie direct to the charges brought against him, Dyce Sombre presented himself for examination before the most eminent physicians of Paris, St. Petersburg, Brussels, and even many first-rate physicians of England, and they unanimously pronounced him sane and capable of managing his own affairs. Strongly supported by these medical opinions Dyce sent in his petitions to the Court of Chancery for an entire supersedeas, but the medical examination held by the Chancery doctors at different periods failed to achieve the desired effect, and the prospect of obtaining redress appeared to Dyce to be an idle dream.

Driven to despair, he now took to a different course. He published in Paris in August 1849 a bulky volume, containing 582 pages, under the heading, *Mr. Dyce Sombre's Refutation of the charge of lunacy brought against him in the Court of Chancery.** The object of the book is

* My best thanks are due both to Mr. O. Couldrey (formerly of Messrs. Gillanders Arbuthnot & Co.) and to

to enable the public to form their own opinion on h's sad case, and he concludes with the following remarks :—

"I believe in the unchastity of my wife, therefore I am a lunatic...........

Thus it is, that by the combined efforts of intrigue, ignorance and misrepresentation, and by the defective state of the English law as regards lunatics, I am debarred from personal liberty in my mother-country ; the management of my property is withheld from me, while it is wasted through negligence or cupidity, and myself cast out as far as practicable from the society of reasonable men, a lunatic among the sane, by the dictum of a few men, who openly profess to set their own wisdom against that of the rest of the world.

And all this is in a country which prides itself upon being the only one in the world, where personal liberty is fairly understood, where a pick-pocket or a murderer will meet with all the tenderness of the law, but where, alas! there is no law for a presumed lunatic, when there are interested parties, whose wishes are that he should remain so" (p. 582).

Weighed down by sorrow and disappointment, Dyce Sombre began to pine away, and at last his health completely gave way. In 1850 he crept over to London

---

Mr. Dasharathi Sanyal, M.A., B.L., (now deceased) for giving me access to this rare and valuable book.

"where he died [1st July, 1851] a lonely and terrible death at Fenton's Hotel, in St. James Street" (*Cal. Rev.* 1880, p. 459). Sixteen years later (August 1867) his remains were carried to Sardhana and laid by the side of his benefactress.

Dyce Sombre was desirous that his hateful wife should have none of his money. "He left a will.........and directed that all his property should be applied to founding a school at Sardhana for boys of mixed parentage, the palace forming the nucleus of the necessary building. To ensure the proving of the will, he made the Chairman and Deputy Chairman of the Court of Directors his executors, with legacies of £10,000 a-piece, but to no purpose. Though these gentlemen fought the case gallantly up to the Queen in Council, the will was negatived in every Court as that of a lunatic; and the whole property devolved upon the widow, as sole heir at law" (*Cal. Rev.* 1880, p. 459).

Mary Anne, the widow of Dyce Sombre, on 8th November 1862 took as her second husband George Cecil Weld, 3rd Baron Forester, and since then became known as Lady Forester. He died on 14th F b. 1886 and she followed him to the grave at the age of eighty, seven years later (7th March, 1893).* She left no issue behind her. During her lifetime she maintained in good order the Sardhana palace, and founded the Forester Hospital and Dispensary at Sardhana, next to St. John's College, with the Begam's money, "for the benefit of the native and other necessitous population of Sardhana and the neighbourhood."† After her death, the palace and the adjoining garden were put up for auction on Monday 28th December 1896, and were purchased by the Catholic Mission of Agra

* For the lineage of Mary Anne, see Burke's *Peerage* (1923), pp. 928, 1956-7.

† The Begam in her will left Rs. 50,000 in trust in favour of Anne Mary, a sister of Dyce Sombre. It was stipulated that should Anne and her husband Col. Troup die without issue, the income of the trust would be appropriated for charitable purposes. It so happened that Col. Troup died on 5th July 1862 without leaving any issue, and his wife, after half a decade, followed suit (18 March 1867). Thereupon Lady Forester, with the principal of the trust, *viz.* Rs. 50,000 created a new trust on 15th April 1876 for the purpose of a hospital and dispensary, which was built at the end of the seventies or beginning of eighties. She herself gave a piece of freehold ground—in all 1,726 sq. yds.—situated at Sardhana, with a house already erected on part thereof, in order that it might be adopted for the purpose. (*Indenture* dated 15-4-1876).

for Rs. 25,000.* The palace is now used for the purpose of an Anglo-Vernacular school and orphanage for Indian Christian boys.

The palace at Sardhana was chiefly remarkable for a collection of some 25 oil-paintings† of the Begam, and her friends, relations and courtiers, drawn by artists of celebrity, such as Jiwan Ram, Beechey of Lucknow, and Melville of Delhi. With the exception of the steel engraving of

---

* The landed possessions at Delhi, Agra and Meerut had in all probability been disposed of by Mrs. Dyce Sombre long before.

† For a description of these paintings, I would refer my readers to Keene and Dyer's articles in the *Cal. Review,* 1880, pp. 460-61; 1894, pp. 312-13. Among them the following deserve a special mention :—(1) The Begam in state chair smoking her *hookah;* (2) The Begam meets Lord Combermere after the fall of Bharatpur; (3) Dyce Sombre painted at Rome; (4) Baron Solaroli and Col. Troup; (5) John Thomas in Mughal costume; (6) H. H. the Begam and Dyce Sombre as a boy; (7) Dr. Thomas Drever, Physician to Her Highness; (8) The Begam presenting a chalice to the Clergy of Sardhana; (9) Fr. Julius Cæsar, first and last Bishop of Sardhana. The first five of these paintings are now in Allahabad Government House.

Lala Sri Ram of Delhi has in his collection an old painting which represents the Begam in male attire with a *hookah* in her hand and a *chopdar* standing by. Two likenesses of the Begam can also be found in the Delhi Museum and a miniature portrait in the frontispiece of vol. I of the first edition of Sleeman's *Rambles*.

Lady Forester, which was sent to her uncle, the rest of the pictures, or most of them, were bought by the local Government in 1895 and these now decorate the walls of Government House, Allahabad.

APPENDIX *E*

PENSION LISTS

There are two lists in the Imperial Record Office, Calcutta, which show the amount of the Begam's monthly expenditure on salaries, pensions, stipends and allowances paid during her lifetime to her dependents etc. The first list* in many instances is obviously not that of pensions but of salaries and allowances, and puts down her total expenditure to Rs. 6,676-11-10 a month.

The second list is principally about pensions† and is divided into five parts as under:—

	Rs.	A.	P.
a. 39 Descendants of old servants, or connections of nobles and respectable native families, connections of the			

* *Pol. Con.* 22 August 1836, No. 35. This list formed the enclosure to a letter, dated 12th March 1836, from the Magistrate of Meerut to the Commissioner.

† *Pol. Con.* 26 September 1836, No. 41. The Magistrate of Meerut, in his letter dated 19th July 1836 to the Commissioner, testified to the authenticity of this pension list in the following terms: "The delay has been occasioned chiefly from the absence of Mr. Dyce Sombre, preventing my obtaining an authentic list; the one now submitted is in original, drawn out from the records of the late Begam's Pay Office and has been compared with the list of pensions actually paid or called over when the arrears were adjusted in February last" (*Pol. Con.* 22 August 1836, No. 40).

		Rs.	A.	P.
	Begam or persons holding situations on her establishment	3,384	12	0
b.	17 Poor Christians ...	146	0	0
c.	69 Widows of Christians who died in the Begam's service	649	0	0
d.	383 Old Hindu and Musalman soldiers and servants pensioned on account of old age and services ...	1,063	6	3
e.	199 Widows of Hindustani soldiers killed in service ...	667	11	6
	Rs.	5,910	13	9

The nature of the division in both the lists is identical, except that the fir t one contains an additional part, *viz.*, "Rs. 176-13-9, being the sum paid monthly to her *rozinadars* and *chandadars*—84 in all." Besides, other differences—such as in the names of the recepients, and their total number and respective amounts—are also noticeable, especially in respect to the first part of the lists. We append below a list of such persons, as played any important part in the life of the Begam, with their respective amounts, etc. from both the lists.

Name.	Date of Grant.	Pay.	Amount of pension.	Why granted.
		Rs.	Rs.	
Paul Solaroli ...	17 Shaban 1246 H. = 1 Feb. 1831	850	850	Brother-in-law of Dyce Sombre.
John Rose Troup ...	28 Zihijja 1246 = 10 June 1831	850	850	Ditto.
Rai Singh Chaudhuri ...	15 Sep 1833	16	16	Old age.
Munshi Gokul Chand ...	26 Rabi-ul-awal 1215 = 18 Aug. 1800	100	40	Old servant.
John Thomas ...	30 Safar 1221 = May 1806 ...	300	300	His father was *Qul-muktear*.
Bishop Pezzoni ...	10 Rabi-us-sani 1243 H. = 1 Nov. 1827 ...	...	300	Bishop of Agra.
R. Richards ...	1 Jamadi-us-sani 1246 H. = 18 Nov. 1830 ...	...	50	Missionary of the Hindustani Chapel, Meerut.
Padre McDonald ...	1 Jany. 1834	...	100	Catholic priest at Meerut.
Maria ...	1 Muharram 1216 H. = 15 May 1801	...	60	George Thomas's wife.
Muhammadi Begam ...	18 Shaban 1238 H. = 30 April 1823	...	20	Her father was the Maratha Resident at Delhi.
Widow of Mons. Pauli	Prior to 1197	Pd. 45 for 3 months	50	Her husband was a Colonel of the Begam.
Bishop Julius Cæsar ...	29 Zihijja 1246 H. = 11 June 1831	400	400	
Major Antoni Reghalini	15 Rabi-us-sani 1226 H. = 9 May 1811	700	200	
Rao Diwan Singh ...	1 Rabi-us-sani 1247 H. = 8 Sep. 1831	300	60	Begam's *diwan*.

NOTE.—*The last three items are taken from the first list.*

APPENDIX F

Funeral Oration on Her Highness The Begam Sombre of Sardhana.

(Delivered on the 27th January, 1839, by the Very Revd N. Wiseman, D.D., Rector of the English College, Rome).

* * * * *

Who is it that, this morning, hath called us together? Is it some noble of the land? One of its sacred princes whose anniversary his friends and family recall to the piety of the faithful? Or is it some distinguished stranger, who, having travelled to this Holy City, has in it found a grave? No, it is one whom no social or political ties connected with us, for whom neither the circumstances of her life, nor of her family would, in a worldly estimate, have procured the celebration here of such solemn obsequies. She was indeed a princess; but many thousands of miles separated her dominions and her interests from Rome. A wide expanse of sea, a wearisome breadth of trackless desert, chains of huge mountains, many kingdoms and various tongues interposed between her and us, seeming to forbid all sympathy, much more all intercourse for any common cause.

But a holier connection than the ordinary bands of human friendship joined her, in spite of distance, with this Apostolic See. Her principality formed one of those very remote points on which the rays, darted from this Centre of Catholic Unity, rested to form churches intimately united with this their Mother. Having embraced the catholic religion, the Princess devoted herself to its maintenance and glory with earnestness and zeal. In her house the venerable Fathers of the Thibetan mission found a home, and every opportunity of discharging their duties. She indeed could say with truth, "Lord, I have loved the glory of Thy house." For she erected a temple of the True God, on a scale of grandeur, unrivalled in modern times in those countries: she lavished upon it all the magnificence, and beauty which native art, generously encouraged, could contribute to its embellishment ; she furnished it with everything necessary for the performance of divine worship upon a princely scale ; and she had the satisfaction of seeing it consecrated and opened, and of submitting to the Holy Father, the plans and drawings of her cathedral before she closed her days. His letters, and the valuable tokens of approval which accompanied them, reached her but a short time previous to her death. Nor did she allow the end of her life, which happened just two years ago, to cut short her pious intentions. A college, established at Sardhana, and endowed by her, will serve to perpetuate her name, and two millions of francs, bequeathed for charitable purposes, will secure her the prayers and blessings of thousands in distress.

And now do we meet here, the extremes of earth to join our voices with theirs, and, in the spirit of religious unity, and in the words of the ancient church, entreat the mercy of God, that "whatever debt she may, through human frailty, have contracted, His compassionate indulgence will forgive." That harbour which she, while living, gave to the preachers of God's truth, Rome, that sends them, now repays to her departed spirit, begging that God will give it refreshment, if not yet attained, in His mansions of bliss ; that submissive and filial obedience, which, when on earth, she paid to the See of Peter, this now gives back in paternal benedictions, and fervent supplications to the Throne of Mercy.

* * * * *

The Princess, whom we commemorate at God's altar, was powerful in her day ; she ruled her dominions with more than woman's arm : she feared not the turmoils and dangers of war, she guided with skill the arduous counsels of peace ; by many she was beloved, by others feared. Yet is she now forever departed ; her strength and wisdom have vanished, her place is filled up by others. Truly, "all flesh is grass, and the glory thereof as the flower of the field" (Is. xl. 6). "The grass is withered, and the flower is fallen." And so shall we who are but flesh also wither, and all the little glory we may have, even as a flower fall and fade away. Oh! here is a glass in which we may look upon our future selves and see to what end all that earth can give must shortly come. For the flattering accents of friends, the whispered supplication for mercy ; for luxurious strains, the stern and solemn tones of funeral music ; for the ample mansion, the narrow vault ; for the soft couch, the strait hard coffin ; for the costly attire, the winding grave clothes ; for precious furniture, dust and corruption. Such is the exchange which we shall one day make, as she of whom we treat hath made it."............(*Sardhana*, pp. 55-64).

BIBLIOGRAPHY

A. *Of first-rate importance*

MARATHI

1. *Dilli-yethil Marathanchin Rajkaranen* (vol. ii. pp. 25, 100, 105, 145).—Hingané or some other Maratha envoy of the Peshwa used to reside at Delhi permanently. The extant portion of the despatches forwarded by them to their masters from time to time, has been published by Rao Bahadur D. B. Parasnis from the Menauli collection. The letters of these writers, conversant as they were with contemporary events, are of great help in composing a history of Upper India as it was at the time. The Maratha Power was then dominant in Hindustan and the value of these Marathi papers cannot be overestimated.

PERSIAN

1. *Ibratnámá* (Prof. Sarkar's Pers. MS.)—The author, Faqir Khair-ud-din Muhammad, was a contemporary of the Begam. He was an influential official and constant companion of Mirza Jahandar (Prince) Jawan Bakht, the son of Shah Alam II. Khair-ud-din was an eye-witness of several of the occurrences described in his work. (Elliot and Dowson, viii. 237, and Qanungo's *Hist. of the Jats*, i. 345).

2. *Waqai-i-Shah Alam Sani* (Prof. Sarkar's Pers. MS.)—This is a diary of news and events at Delhi kept from day to day. There are many gaps in it, but from what is left of the manuscript we find a brief recital of the events from 1739 to 1799, *i.e.*, from the sack of Delhi by Nadir Shah to the eve of the British entry into Delhi under Lord Lake. The writer was an inhabitant of the city, and his work is an absolutely contemporary chronicle of the events and rumours of Delhi. (For a full discussion of this source, see *Proceedings of the Indian Historical Records Commission,* iii. 5-6).

3. A biography of the Begam written in Persian verse is preserved in the British Museum (Dr. Rieu's *B. M. Cat. of Persian MSS.*, ii. 724*a,* Add. 25830). It was composed by Lala Gokul Chand, the *Khas Munshi* of the Begam, in 1824. The author writes to say that he thought it necessary to compose this book as the biography of the Begam in prose by *Munshi* Jai Singh Rai had been lost. I have a facsimile taken by rotary process of the first four pages of this manuscript, but this portion reveals nothing of any historical interest. We should not however pronounce a judgment on it before examining the remainder of the MS.

ENGLISH

1. *Imperial Records.*—The search, conducted by me in the Imperial Record Office, Calcutta, revealed at least three to four hundred Consultations and Despatches to the Court of Directors—both Political and Secret—between the years 1791 and 1839, having direct reference to the Begam. These

documents throw a flood of light on her jagir, her administration, her private possessions, the strength of her army, duty detail, the annual income of her principality, the transit duties levied both on land and water, her charitable bequests ; the names, dates of entry, salaries etc. of those officers, relations and dependents who enjoyed her pensions or stipends, etc.

A few of the Begam's letters to the British Government were in English, but most of them were written in Persian, and these original letters are now in the Imperial Record Office. It is of interest to note that according to the practice of the age these Persian letters were left undated, but the envelopes bore the dates of writing in Hijra. Such envelopes have in most cases been preserved with the original letters.

Translations of the Persian letters, both received and issued by the British Government, have also been preserved in the Record Office with great care. These translations have on them the dates of receipt of the letters at Fort William, instead of the dates of writing given on the envelopes.

2. *Panjab Secretariat Records.*—All letters, exchanged between the Begam and the Company, generally passed through the Resident at Delhi, who used to preserve copies of them in the Residency. Soon after the Sepoy Mutiny it was found necessary to transfer all records in the Delhi Residency to the Panjab. After a prolonged search elsewhere I have at last been able to trace, among the records of the Panjab Secretariat, a copy of the Begam's will, which is a very important document, giving full

details of the disposition of her vast personal property.

There is reason to believe that further search among the Secretariat records may lead to the discovery of more useful information.

3. Mr. Dyce Sombre's *Refutation of the charge of Lunacy brought against him in the Court of Chancery.* Paris, 1849. The author of this rare book, Mr. Dyce Sombre, was the adopted son and heir of the Begam. In some respects this book is an invaluable help to every student of the Begam's biography, as it contains such valuable documents as her will (part), her deed of gift, her agreement with the Company, an account of her personal landed property and its income, and several other important matters. There are in it copies of a considerable number of the E. I. Company's despatches which I could not trace even in the Imperial Record Office, Calcutta.

4. *Military Memoirs of Mr. George Thomas,* compiled and arranged from Mr. Thomas's original Documents, by Wm. Francklin. Calcutta 1803.

The material of this book was derived chiefly from Thomas's own narrations. It gives us an insight into the Begam's mode of living, her army, *jagir,* etc.

5. *Rambles & Recollections of an Indian Official,* by Major-Genl. Sir W. H. Sleeman, 2nd ed. (2 vols. Westminster, 1893). See vol. ii. (1st ed. published in 1844).

Comparatively speaking Sleeman's account of the Begam is the most reliable. He was her contemporary and had the best possible opportunities of ascertaining the truth.

6. (*a*) *The Despatches, Minutes of Correspondence of the Marquis Wellesley, K. G.,* during his administration in India. Ed. by R. Montgomery Martin. London, 1837 (5 vols.)—See iii. 214, 229, 243.

(*b*) *Privy Council Judgments* on Appeals from India, edited by Pandit Pran Nath Saraswati and Bidhu Bhusan Banerjee, (iii. 1871-78) ; pp. 1-15, 717-21.

(*c*) *Judgments of the Privy Council* on Appeals from India, from 1831-1867. D. Sutherland. Calcutta 1867 ; pp. 287-90.

The first two volumes are chiefly valuable for sundry copies of correspondence which have been printed in relation to the treaty concluded between the British and the Begam.

FRENCH

1. *Le Nabob Rene Madec,* par Emile Barbe, Paris, 1894. Most valuable for a French comrade's brief account of General Sombre in his last year.

2. *Pondicherry Records.* Memoire annexed to M. de Bussy's letter to Marechal de Castries, dated 3rd March 1784, entered as No. 423 in the *Catalogue des Manuscrits des......l'Inde Francaise,* tome 1, (1922), p. 153. (A translation of this memoir has been published in the *Modern Review,* Sep. 1925).

B. *Of second-rate importance*

1. *Shah-Aulum*, by Capt. Wm. Francklin, 2nd ed. Allahabad, 1915. (1st ed. published in 1798).

Francklin, a contemporary of the Begam, obtained his informations from Persian sources. Some of the incidents, connected with her life, have been described in detail in this book.

2. (*a*) Major Wm. Thorn's *Memoir of the War in India*, conducted by Genl. Lord Lake and Major-Genl. Sir Arthur Wellesley. London 1818. See pp. 274, 331-32, 385, 386, 387, 480, 509.

(*b*) *A Tour through the Upper Provinces of Hindostan; comprising a period between the Years 1804 and 1814*, by A. D. [Mrs. A. Dearie]. London 1823.

(*c*) *Narrative of a Journey through the Upper Provinces of India*, by Rt. Rev. Reginald Heber, D.D., Lord Bishop of Calcutta. London 1828. (2 vols). See i. 543.

(*d*) *Pen and Pencil Sketches*, being the Journal of a Tour in India, by Capt. Mundy (Late Aide-de-camp to Lord Combermere). London 1832, vol. i.

(*e*) *Tours in Upper India*, by Major Archer, Late Aide-de-camp to Lord Combermere, 2 vols. London 1833. See vol. i.

(*f*) *Letters from India*, by Victor Jacquemont, (2 vols.) London 1834. See ii. 246-47.

(*g*) *First Impressions and Studies from Nature in Hindustan*, by Thomas Bacon (2 vols.), London 1837. See vol. ii.

Thorn gives a brief but reliable account of the Begam. Mrs. Deane, Heber, Mundy, Archer, Jacquemont and Bacon were all visitors to the Begam's Court and have recorded mostly bazar gossip. They are reliable only so far as they describe things they actually saw, *viz.*, the buildings, parks, and condition of the Sardhana principality, the Begam's mode of living and character, her army etc.

3. *Military Memoir of Lt.-Col. J. Skinner, C.B.*, by J. Baillie Fraser. London 1851 (2 vols.)—see i. ch. x. Based chiefly on Thomas, Francklin, and Scott's *Hist. of the Deccan.*

4. *Statistical, Descriptive and Historical Account of the North Western Provinces of India*, by E. T. Atkinson. Allahabad 1875. Vols. ii. & iii.

In the second volume an account is given of the leading events connected with the life of the Begam, based principally on Thomas, Sleeman, Francklin, Archer, Mundy, Bacon and Skinner. The third volume gives an account of the Begam's *jagir*, military forces, etc. The portion dealing with revenue has been written with the help of T. C. Plowden's *Settlement Report of 1840* of the Meerut District.

5. *Sardhana and its Begum*, by Rev. W. Keegan, D.D. Revised, enlarged and illustrated by Rev. Fr. Christopher, O.C., Agra 1921, 5th ed. The first edition of this pamphlet was most probably

published in 1879 or 1880. It is a compilation, and Sleeman has been largely drawn upon.

6. *European Military Adventurers of Hindustan from 1784 to 1803,* compiled by Herbert Compton. London 1892. Based chiefly on Sleeman and Thomas.

C. *Chiefly abstracts of second-rate materials*

1. "Sketches of the Remarkable Living Characters in India. No. 1. Col. Gardiner.—The Begum Sumroo." *The Asiatic Journal and* Monthly Register, vol. xv—N. Series; Septr.-Decr. 1834; pp. 144-151. Based on Mrs. Deane and Archer.

2. *Le General de Boigne,* par Victor de Saint-Genis (1873). Utterly unreliable. Full of false rumours.

3. *Memoirs and Correspondence of Field-Marshall Viscount Combermere,* by Viscountess Combermere. London 1866. See ii. 160-170, 195.

4. G. R. C. Williams: *Historical Sketches*—The Sikhs in the Upper Doab, pub. in *Calcutta Review,* No. cxxi (1875), p. 54.

5. H. G. Keene:—(*a*) "Sardhana:—The Seat of the Sombres—Its Past and Present"—*Calcutta Review,* 1880; vol. lxx, pp. 445-66.

(b) "George Thomas," *Calcutta Review,* 1880; pp. 597-618.

(c) *Hindustan under Free Lances 1770-1820,* London 1907.

6. "Romance and Reality of Indian Life"—*Calcutta Review*, 1884, pp. 417-22.

7. "The Begum of Sardhana"—A. Saunder Dyer, (Late) Chaplain of Meerut. *Calcutta Review*, 1894 April ; pp. 310-26.

8. "A Bishop in Partibus"—J. W. Sherer. *Gentleman's Magazine*, vol. 280 (1896) ; pp. 466-69.

9. J. J. Higginbotham's *Men whom India has known*. See "Sumroo" (pp. 406-8), 2nd ed. Madras 1874. (1st ed. 1870).

10. "A Calcutta Benefactress"—G. H. [G. Huddleston], *Bengal Past and Present* (Hist. Society's Journal) 1907 ; pp. 137-47.

11. *Memoir of the Life and Military Services of Viscount Lake*, by Col. Hugh Pearse. London, 1908 ; pp. 252-53.

12. "From Slave to Princess"—Cecil L. Burns. *The Times of India, Annual* 1923.

A REQUEST

I shall be thankful if any reader informs me where I can consult the following books which I have not yet been able to read :—

1. *The Heirs of Dyce Sombre V. the Indian Government.* The History of a suit during thirty years between a private individual and the Government of India, Westminster, 1865. 8°.
2. In the Prerogative Court of Canterbury. Dyce Sombre against Troup, Solaroli intervening, and Prinsep, and the Hon. East India Company, also intervening. In the goods of D. O. Dyce Sombre, ...deceased. Scripts — pleadings — answers — interrogatories — minutes — and exhibits. (Depositions of witnesses). 2 vols. 8°. [Privately printed] London [1855 ?]
3. *Reports of Revenue Settlement*, N.-W. P., vol. I.

INDEX

Abdul Ahad Khan (Majd-ud-daula), ingratiates himself with Sombre, 8; his growing reluctance to back Sombre's interests, 10.

Agha Wanns, 67.

Ajmir, 30.

Akbar (the Emperor), 2.

Akbar (Mirza), the Prince Regent, 42-43; becomes Emperor, 186.

Aligarh, 12.

Ambaji Dhara Rao (Maratha), 30*n*, 161.

Antoine, bandmaster of the Begam, 181.

Anwar-ud-din, Nawab of the Karnatak, 3.

Anupshahr, 49, 73.

Appa Khande Rao (Khande Rao Hari), employs Geo. Thomas, 42, 43, 161.

Asaf-ud-daula (the Nawab Wazir), 54.

Aurangzib (the Emperor), 2.

Ballamgarh, 22.

Bapu Sindhia, 62, 65.

Barlow (Sir George), 115.

Barsana, battle of, 7.

The Begam (wife of Genl. Sombre *alias* Samru), ancestry and early life, 14-15; is married to Genl. Sombre, 16; a convert to Roman Catholicism, 18; baffles the design of Ghulam Qadir upon Delhi, 23; heroic conduct at the siege of Gokulgarh, 27; secures pardon for Najaf Quli, 29; her new *jagir*, 29*n*; protects Ambaji Maratha, 30*n*; her help sought by Prince Jahandar Shah, 31; her interview with the historian Khair-ud-din Allahabadi, 32; love intrigues, 38; secret marriage with a French officer, 39; her new embarrassments, 41; political correspondence with the English, 44-45; meditates revenge on Geo. Thomas, 46; a mutiny in her army, 48; her petition to Sir John Shore, 51*n*; stabs herself to escape capture, 56; a prisoner in the hands of the rebels, 57; appeals to Geo. Thomas for rescue, 62; regains her liberty and status, 65; grateful recognition of Thomas's services, 66-67*n*; perpetuates the loving memory of Sombre, 68; her friendly dealings with the British, 74-75; sends an agent to Lord Lake, 84; unfairly treated by Wellesley, 91; her alleged treachery, 94; her attitude to the belligerent Powers, 98; gets back her principality, 104; makes provisions for her dependents, 114; her pious activity, 117; her will, 119; retires from public duties, 120; her gift to the Pope and donations to the Church of England, 121-122; endowment of her religious institutions, 124-126; gifts to Hindu and Muslim institutions, 127; her death, 127; story about the granting of a lease of five years' life by a Muslim saint, 128; touching scene at her burial, 130; extent of her *jagir*, 134-138; her revenue, 140-142; expenses of her administration, 143; efficiency of her army, 144; strength of her army corps, 148-149; military expenditure, 151; personal property and palaces, 152; administration and policy, 159; diplomatic triumph over Wellesley and Lake, 162; beneficent rule, 164-165; adverse criticisms on her administration refuted, 166-167; burial alive of the slave-girls, 168-170; her personal charms, 177; courtesy and liberality, 178-179; a born ruler of men yet a woman too, 185-187.

Bentinck (Lord William), his high appreciation of the Begam's virtues, 171.

Bhanga Singh (Sikh chief), 73.

Bidar Bakht (Prince), 34.

Buxar, the battle of, 6.

Chandernagar, French colony, 4.

Combermere (Field-marshal), 146, 195.

Cornwallis (Lord), 103.

Danishmand Khan, 3.

Daulat Rao Sindhia, succeeds Mahadji, 42*n*; decline of his power, 77; war with the English, 81; deserted by the Begam's troops, 83.

Deeg, 100.

Delhi, first siege by Ghulam Qadir, 21-25; second siege and capture, 34.

Dhokul Singh, 101*n*.

Dyce (Col. G. A.), his children by Zafar-yab's daughter, 189; dismissed from Begam's service, 190; his death, 196.

Dyce Sombre (David Ochterlony Dyce), adopted by the Begam, 68, 190; made her heir under a will, 120; faithfully carries out the Begam's wishes, 131*n*; erects a monument in memory of the Begam, 158; character and education of, 191; journey to Europe, 196; unhappy marriage in England, 197; a prisoner by the conspiracy of his wife, 198; escapes to Paris, 199; writes his *Refutation* to prove his sanity, 200; miserable death and will, 158, 202.

Ellis (the English factor), executed, 6.

The English: victories over the Marathas, 4; seek vengeance upon Sombre, 9, 11; their help sought by Mirza Akbar, 43; relations with the Begam, 74-75; a clash with the Maratha Powers, 80; their fears about the Begam, 99; terms of the treaty with the Begam, 106.

Faridabad, 31.

Farrukhabad, 49.

Fr. Gregorio (Rev.), a Carmelite monk, performs Begam's secret marriage ceremony, 40; acts as her envoy to the English, 44.

George Thomas, early life, 2; rapid rise in Begam's service, 18; a disappointed lover resigns his service, 38; other versions of the story of his resignation, 38*n*, 39*n*, 40*n*; enters Maratha service, 41; plunders portions of Begam's territories, 42; chivalrous response to the appeal of the captive Begam, 64; leaves his wife and children to Begam's care, 66.

Ghulam Qadir (Ruhela), attacks Delhi, 21; outwitted by the Begam, 23; sues for peace, 25; his second siege of and atrocities at Delhi, 34-35; his captivity and horrible mutilation, 36.

Gokulgarh, 26.

Gregorio, *see* Fr. Gregorio.

Gurgin Khan, general of Mir Qasim, employs Sombre, 4.

Guthrie (G. D.), Collector of Saharanpur, liberated by the Begam from Sher Singh, 98-99, 162.

Haidar Ali, Mysore Sultan, 1.

Hastings, W., 72.

Holkar (Tukoji), 4.

Holkar (Jaswant Rao), alleged conspiracy of the Begam with, 93, 93*n*; war with the English, 97; tries to win over the Begam, 98.

Jahandar Shah (Mirza Jawan Bakht), seeks Begam's help, 31; his disappointment and death, 33, 161.

Jalalpur, 154.

Jawahir Singh (the Jat Rajah), takes Sombre in his service, 6.

Jhujjar, 46.

Khatauli, 63.

Khair-ud-din (the historian), serves as an envoy of Prince Jahandar Shah, 31; his witty conversation with the Begam, 32.

Khande Rao, *see* Appa.

Khirwa, 55, 154.

Kuchait Singh, Sikh *faujdar* of Karnal, 9.

Kutana, birth-place of Begam Samru.

Lake (Lord), Commander-in-chief, instructed to negotiate with the Begam, 81; his demands, 82; letters to the Begam, 87; his injudicious kiss, 184.

Legois, a French officer, 48.

Levassoult, a French officer supplants Geo. Thomas in the Begam's affections, 38; secret marriage with the Begam, 39; his aristocratic *hauteur*, 40; open enmity with Thomas, 46; applies for an asylum in the British territory, 49; correspondence with the English, 50; attempts flight with the Begam, 54; shoots himself to death, 56.

Lutf Ali Khan, father of Begam Samru, 14, 15.

Mahadji Sindhia, Maratha statesman, 1; adopts European method of warfare, 4; suffers a reverse in Rajputana, 20; temporary eclipse of his power, 30; sends an army to recover Delhi, 35; punishes Ghulam Qadir, 36; his death, 42.

Manzur Ali (the *nazir*), intrigues with Ghulam Qadir, 21; his advice to Ghulam Qadir, 25; turns the Emperor's heart against the Marathas, 30; poisons Emperor's mind against the eldest prince, 33; admits Ghulam Qadir inside the citadel, 34; horrible death, 37.

Maria, wife of Geo. Thomas, 67.

Mary Anne, marriage with Dyce Sombre, 197; conspiracy against her husband, 198; suspected of adultery, 201; second marriage, 202; founds Forester Hospital at Sardhana, 203.

Minto (Lord), 115, 116.

Mir Qasim, 6.

M. Montigny, a French officer and candidate for the Begam's hand, 17*n*.

Najaf Khan (Zulfiqar-ud-daula), the statesman and soldier, 1; detaches Sombre from Jat service, 7; campaigns against the Jats, 10.

Najaf Quli Khan, besieged at Gokulgarh, 26; censured by the Begam, 27; seeks Begam's mediation, 29.

Nawal Singh Jat, 7.

Nizam-ud-din (Shah), deputy of Sindhia, 20; defeated by Ghulam Qadir, 21; retreats to Ballamgarh, 22.

Panipat, 9, 10.
Parashuram Bhao Patvardhan, 1.
Patna, massacre of, 6.
Pauli, a German officer, succeeds Sombre to the command, is decapitated by Md. Beg Hamadani, 17.
M. Perron, general of Sindhia tries to seduce Begam's troops, 77, 108.
Pratap Singh (Maharajah of Jaipur), heads a coalition against Mahadji Sindhia, 20, 22.

Qandahari Khan, 34.

Ranah Khan, 35.
Ranjit Singh (Lahor chief), an ally of the Begam, 85, 181, 181*n*.
Raymond, French captain, 2.
Rene Madec, French captain, 2.
Rewari, 26.

Saharanpur, 25, 85, 98.
Saleur (Jean), his fidelity to the Begam, 61, 66; commands Sardhana brigade at Assaye, 82; ordered to join the English camp, 83; his illness, 84.
Sardhana, foundation of the principality of, 12; usurped by Zafar-yab, 57; recovered by the Begam, 66; under British protection, 72; restored to the Begam, 104; annexed by the British after Begam's death, 131; glimpses of the Court of, 176; Court festivities at, 182; pictures at the palace of, 204.
Shah Alam II (the Emperor), incompetency of, 8; grants Sonipat and Panipat to Genl. Sombre, 9; invests the Begam with the command of her husband's corps, 17; his helplessness, 22; marches against Najaf Quli, 26; a tool in the hand of an eunuch, 30, 33; blinded by Ghulam Qadir, 34; his high regard for the Begam's abilities, 160.

Shakir Shah, a Muslim saint who died for the Begam, 128.
Sher Singh, 98.
Shuja-ud-daula (Nawab), 9.
Sindhia, *see* **Mahadji** and **Bapu**.
Solaroli (Paul), marries Anne—sister of Dyce Sombre, 189.
Sonipat, 9.

Thomas (George), see under "George".
Troup (Capt. Rose), marries Georgiana—sister of Dyce Sombre, 189.

Verne, Jules, author of *Begam's Fortune*, 188.
Victoria (Queen), certain claims made over to by Dyce Sombre, 194.
Visage (Mons.), French commandant, 13.

Walter Reinhardt (*alias* Sombre or Samru), a German adventurer, 2; early career in French service, 4; character, 5; age, 5*n*; plays the butcher at Patna, 6; joins the service of Rajah Jawahir Singh Jat, 6; picks up Begam Samru during Jawahir's siege of Delhi, 14; tempting offers from the Mughal Court, 7; interview with the Emperor Shah Alam II, 8; complains of the poor income of his *jagir*, 10; attaches himself to the party of Mirza Najaf Khan, 11; period of his service with Najaf Khan, 11*n*; appointed governor of Agra, 12; death and burial, 13; strength of his army corps at the time of his death, 17*n*.
Wanus, *see* Agha W.
Warren Hastings, 72.
Wellesley (Marquis of), his letter to the Begam, 81; policy with regard to the Begam's principality, 86, 89; his dubious policy, a blunder, 96; his suspicious and unfriendly attitude to the Begam, 102-103.

Zafar-yab Khan (Reynard or Sombre), son of Genl. Somore by another Muhammadan wife, 13; becomes a convert to the Roman Catholic faith, 18; invited by the rebellious troops of the Begam to assume their lead, 49; becomes master of Sardhana, 57; his forged letters to the English, 58-59; his marriage, 188; maternal grandfather of Dyce Sombre, 189; surprised by Geo. Thomas, 64; his imprisonment and death, 66.

Zaman Shah, 161.

ADDITIONS

BEGAM SAMRU'S DETHRONEMENT

The following passage in Governor-General Shore's Bengal Political letter to the Court of Directors, dated 9th January 1796, furnishes the true cause of the revolt which led to the dethronement of the Begam :—

> "55. A desertion of two battalions of sepoys in the service of the Begam, widow of Samru, having taken place, in consequence of her husband, M. Le Vassoult, attempting to supersede the officer in command of them in favor of his own nephew, this corps marched from their station near Delhi to that city ; and put themselves under the orders of Zafar-yab Khan, the son of Samru by a former wife, whom the Begam had excluded from the succession to his father's jagir. In consequence of this revolt, the Begam and her husband quitted Sardhana and fled towards the Maratha districts, but were pursued and soon overtaken, and M. Le Vassoult, finding he could not escape, shot himself. The Begam was carried back a prisoner to Sardhana, and Zafar-yab Khan, who also proceeded thither, on being informed of the above events, is, we conclude, now in possession of the jagir."

REVENUE OF SARDHANA PARGANA

In a letter from Begam Samru, received by the Governor-General on 20th October, 1831, we find the following passage :—

> "The pargana of Sardhana contains 102 mouzas both Usli and Dakhilli, the annual revenue of which is at least Rs. 1,50,000, together with transit duties attached to the said pargana." (*Pol. Procdgs.* 25 Nov. 1831, No. 10).

SARDHANA PICTURES

Of the Sardhana pictures the Indian Institute at Oxford possesses the portraits of Fr. Julius Cæsar, the first and last Bishop of Sardhana, Dr. Drever, the Begam's physician, and the two brothers-in-law of Dyce Sombre—Baron Paul Solaroli and Col. John Rose Troup.